Southern Living®

dinner in a dish

100 CALORIES
100 CALORIES
300 CALORIES
100 CALORIES
ALMONDS
MILK

Easy One-Recipe Meals
for Casseroles, Slow Cookers, Skillet Suppers, Pizza, Pasta, and More

Oxmoor House®

ISBN-13: 978-0-8487-3349-0
ISBN-10: 0-8487-3349-5
Library of Congress Control Number: 2009937188

Printed in the United States of America
First Printing 2010

Oxmoor House, Inc.

VP, Publishing Director: Jim Childs
Editorial Director: Susan Payne Dobbs
Brand Manager: Daniel Fagan
Senior Editor: Rebecca Brennan
Managing Editor: Laurie S. Herr

Dinner in a Dish

Editor: Susan Ray
Project Editor: Georgia Dodge
Senior Designer: Emily Albright Parrish
Director, Test Kitchens:
Elizabeth Tyler Austin
Assistant Directors, Test Kitchens:
Julie Christopher, Julie Gunter
Test Kitchens Professionals:
Wendy Ball, Allison E. Cox,
Victoria E. Cox, Margaret Monroe Dickey,
Callie Nash, Kathleen Royal Phillips,
Catherine Crowell Steele, Alyson Moreland Haynes,
Leah Van Deren
Photography Director: Jim Bathie
Senior Photo Stylist: Kay E. Clarke
Associate Photo Stylist: Katherine Eckert Coyne
Assistant Photo Stylist: Mary Louise Menendez
Production Managers: Theresa Beste-Farley,
Tamara Nall Wilder

Contributors

Compositor: Teresa Cole
Copy Editor: Dolores Hydock
Proofreader: Catherine Fowler
Indexer: Mary Ann Laurens
Interns: Christine Taylor Boatwright, Allison Sperando,
Caitlin Watzke

Southern Living®

Executive Editor: Scott Jones
Food Editor: Shannon Sliter Satterwhite
Senior Writer: Donna Florio
Senior Food Editors: Shirley Harrington, Mary Allen Perry
Senior Recipe Editor: Ashley Leath
Test Kitchen Director: Lyda Jones Burnette
Assistant Test Kitchen Director: Rebecca Kracke Gordon
Test Kitchen Specialists/Food Styling: Marian Cooper
Cairns, Vanessa McNeil Rocchio
Test Kitchen Professionals: Norman King, Pam Lolley,
Angela Sellers
Senior Photographers: Ralph Anderson, Jennifer Davick
Photographer: Beth Dreiling Hontzas
Senior Photo Stylist: Buffy Hargett
Editorial Assistant: Pat York

To order additional publications, call 1-800-765-6400
or 1-800-491-0551

For more books to enrich your life, visit
oxmoorhouse.com

To search, savor, and share thousands of recipes,
visit **myrecipes.com**

Cover: Saucy Manicotti (page 65)

contents

meal PLANNING

Tips for an Organized Kitchen

1 Store wooden spoons, rubber and metal spatulas, tongs, wire whisks, cooking spoons, and kitchen shears in a jar near your cooktop and mixing center. Store pot holders close to the oven, cooktop, and microwave for quick access.

2 Place bottles and boxes in your cupboard on a pullout tray where you can easily see the ingredients that you need.

3 Stock your kitchen with must-have cooking gadgets and appliances to save time and energy (see ideas on opposite page). Purchase duplicates of things you use most often, such as measuring cups and spoons.

4 Save counterspace by using stackable canisters for flour, sugar, and coffee. Keep a set of measuring cups and spoons in the flour and sugar containers.

Must-Have Equipment

Food processors will chip, shred, and grate for you. Use them to chop several batches of vegetables at one time and freeze them for later use.

Slow cookers allow you to safely cook a meal while you're away from home. The low temperature gently simmers food for hours unattended, allowing you to come home from a busy day to a delicious dinner.

Salad spinners are great for quickly rinsing greens. And salads make the perfect accompaniment for one-dish meals.

Measuring cups and spoons come in graduated sizes. Select a set of metal or plastic measuring cups for dry ingredients. They come in sizes of 1 cup, ½ cup, ⅓ cup, and ¼ cup. Measuring spoons also come in plastic or metal and graduate in size from ⅛ teaspoon to 1 tablespoon.

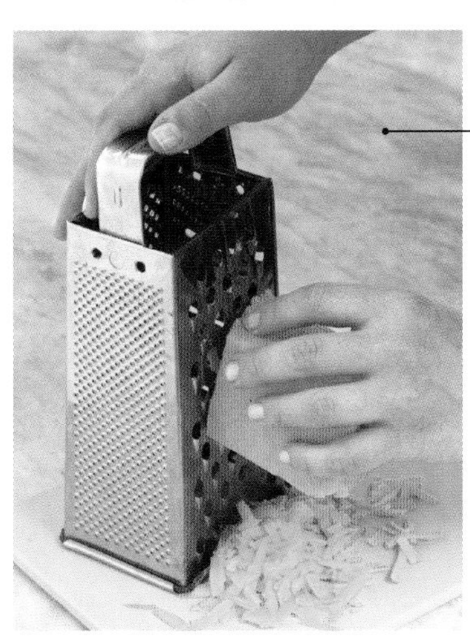

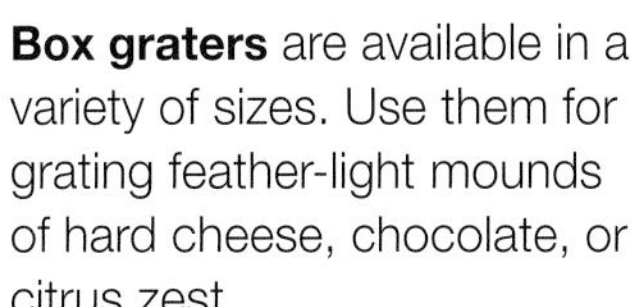

Box graters are available in a variety of sizes. Use them for grating feather-light mounds of hard cheese, chocolate, or citrus zest.

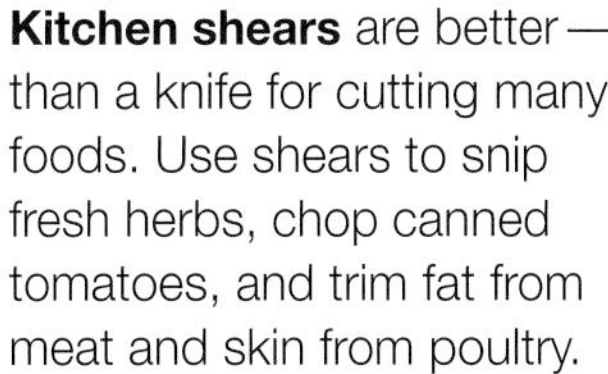

Kitchen shears are better than a knife for cutting many foods. Use shears to snip fresh herbs, chop canned tomatoes, and trim fat from meat and skin from poultry.

Menu Planning Hints

Good-quality convenience foods save time: For example, make your special potato casserole, but combine it with deli roasted chicken, a frozen ready-to-steam vegetable mix, and pop-and-bake rolls.

Jump-start your next meal: Grill extra chicken to add to a salad, turn into chicken salad, or use for quesadillas another night. Double a spaghetti sauce recipe, and freeze the surplus in single-serving portions.

Oven management: If all dishes are cooked in the oven at different temperatures, rethink the menu plan.

Dining in shifts: If family members eat at different times, you need foods that hold well. If using the microwave, reheat using 60% to 70% power. It takes longer, but the heating will be more even, and the food will taste fresher.

The dish on casseroles: Stock casseroles in your freezer without tying up your dishes. Line each dish with heavy-duty aluminum foil. Cover and freeze finished casserole 2 to 3 hours. Lift the frozen casserole from the dish and freeze in a zip-top plastic freezer bag.

Cleanup: To avoid hand-cleaning pans, line baking sheets with parchment paper and cook veggies in microwave-safe serving dishes.

Grocery Shopping Strategies

Our Test Kitchens Professionals shop a lot in order to prepare more than 6,000 recipes each year. Here's how they suggest you get up and down the supermarket aisles in a hurry.

1 While you're making your grocery list, scan the recipes that you plan to make for the week to determine what on-hand ingredients you already have and any special cooking equipment you'll need. Be sure to buy extras of pantry staples that you use frequently.

2 Organize your grocery list by category: meat, dairy, produce, canned goods, frozen foods, breads, and so on. Make a template for your grocery list on your computer. Establish a set of abbreviations for commonly purchased items to use as shorthand on your list: pt (paper towels), chix (chicken), mjc (Monterey Jack cheese), etc.

3 Shop for nonperishables first (usually the aisles), and then move to the perimeter of the store to pick up produce, meats, refrigerated foods, dairy products, and frozen items.

4 Put nonperishables on one side of the shopping cart and perishables on the other. At the checkout stand, group nonrefrigerated items together and refrigerated items together. This way, like items will be bagged together for easy unpacking at home.

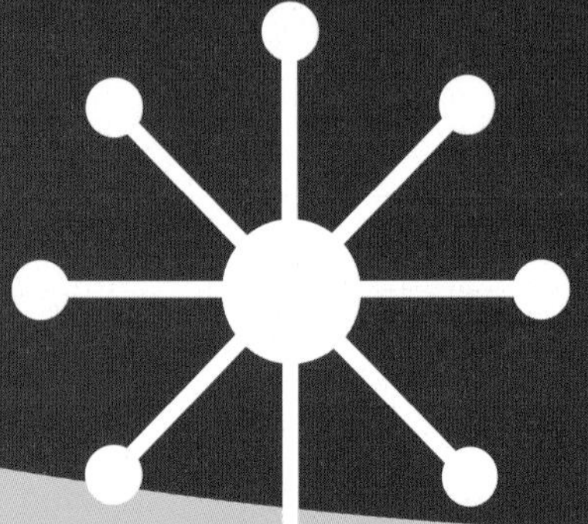

not just

BREAKFAST

Cajun Omelet

MAKES 4 servings • **HANDS-ON TIME:** 25 min. • **TOTAL TIME:** 25 min.

- 5 tsp. butter, divided
- 1¼ cups sliced andouille sausage
- 2 small plum tomatoes, seeded and chopped
- ½ medium onion, chopped
- ½ medium-size red bell pepper, chopped
- 1 celery rib, chopped
- 1 tsp. minced garlic
- 1 tsp. Creole seasoning, divided
- 12 large eggs
- 1 Tbsp. chopped fresh parsley
- Vegetable cooking spray
- 1½ cups (6 oz.) shredded Monterey Jack cheese
- Hot sauce

1. Melt 1 tsp. butter in a 10-inch nonstick heavy skillet over medium-high heat; add sausage, and cook, stirring occasionally, 6 to 7 minutes or until sausage is well browned. Add tomatoes, next 4 ingredients, and ½ tsp. Creole seasoning. Cook 5 to 7 minutes or until vegetables are tender and most of liquid has evaporated. Remove from skillet.
2. Whisk together eggs, parsley, and remaining ½ tsp. Creole seasoning.
3. Melt 1 tsp. butter in skillet coated with cooking spray over medium heat, rotating pan to evenly coat bottom. Pour one-fourth of egg mixture into skillet. As egg mixture starts to cook, gently lift edges of omelet with a spatula, and tilt pan so uncooked portion flows underneath. Cook until almost set (about 1 minute). Cover skillet, and cook 1 minute.
4. Sprinkle 1 side of omelet with one-fourth each sausage mixture and cheese. Fold omelet in half over filling. Slide omelet onto a serving plate; cover with aluminum foil to keep warm. Repeat procedure 3 times with remaining butter, egg mixture, sausage mixture, and cheese. Serve with hot sauce.

Farmer's Oven-Baked Omelet

Farmer's cheese is a mild, part-skim, semisoft cheese available in 8-oz. rounds. Havarti or Monterey Jack cheese may be substituted.

MAKES 10 to 12 servings • **HANDS-ON TIME:** 20 min. • **TOTAL TIME:** 50 min.

- 12 large eggs
- ½ cup sour cream
- 2 Tbsp. chopped fresh thyme
- 1 tsp. salt
- ¾ tsp. freshly ground pepper
- ¼ tsp. baking powder
- 2 Tbsp. butter
- 6 small plum tomatoes, seeded and chopped
- 2 cups (8 oz.) shredded farmer's cheese
- ½ cup chopped fresh basil
- Garnish: fresh basil leaves

1. Preheat oven to 350°. Beat first 6 ingredients at medium speed with an electric mixer 2 to 3 minutes or until well blended.
2. Melt butter in a 12-inch ovenproof skillet; add egg mixture.
3. Bake at 350° for 15 minutes. Remove from oven; sprinkle with tomatoes, cheese, and chopped basil. Return to oven, and bake 15 to 20 more minutes or until set. Garnish, if desired; serve immediately.

Spinach, Cheddar, and Bacon Omelet: Substitute 1 (10-oz.) package frozen, thawed, and well-drained chopped spinach for thyme. Omit farmer's cheese and fresh basil. Top with 2 cups (8 oz.) shredded Cheddar cheese and ½ cup cooked, crumbled bacon.

Garden Omelet

MAKES 2 servings • **HANDS-ON TIME:** 16 min. • **TOTAL TIME:** 16 min.

- **1 small tomato, seeded and chopped**
- **1 small zucchini, chopped**
- **1 small yellow squash, chopped**
- **¼ cup chopped onion**
- **¼ cup chopped green bell pepper**
- **¼ cup sliced fresh mushrooms**
- **Vegetable cooking spray**
- **4 large eggs**
- **1 to 2 tsp. hot sauce**
- **¼ tsp. salt**
- **½ cup (2 oz.) shredded sharp Cheddar cheese**
- **1 Tbsp. chopped fresh parsley**

1. Sauté first 6 ingredients in a 10-inch nonstick skillet coated with cooking spray over medium-high heat 9 minutes or until liquid evaporates; remove from skillet, and set aside. Wipe skillet clean.
2. Whisk together eggs, hot sauce, and salt; pour into skillet coated with cooking spray. As egg mixture starts to cook, gently lift edges with a spatula, and tilt pan so uncooked portion flows underneath.
3. Spoon vegetables onto egg, and sprinkle with shredded cheese. Fold in half, and transfer to a serving plate; sprinkle with chopped parsley.

How To Make an Omelet

Whip up the perfect omelet for dinner—a nonstick skillet is the only equipment you need. Use the nonstick skillet to first sauté all the veggies and other ingredients that you plan to use in your omelet. Once cooked, set that aside and whisk together the eggs and other ingredients. Pour into the skillet. As egg mixture starts to cook, gently lift edges of omelet with a spatula, and tilt pan so uncooked egg mixture flows underneath, cooking until almost set (about 1 minute). Cover skillet, and cook 1 minute. Fold omelet in half. Slide cooked omelet onto a serving plate.

Cornbread Omelet

MAKES 5 servings • **HANDS-ON TIME:** 20 min. • **TOTAL TIME:** 20 min.

- **¾ lb. chorizo sausage, casings removed (about 3 links)**
- **6 Tbsp. butter, divided**
- **3 green onions, chopped**
- **1 small red bell pepper, chopped**
- **2 jalapeño peppers, minced**
- **1 cup self-rising white cornmeal mix**
- **½ cup buttermilk**
- **½ cup milk**
- **¼ cup all-purpose flour**
- **1 large egg, lightly beaten**
- **Vegetable cooking spray**
- **1 cup (4 oz.) shredded Mexican cheese blend**

1. Sauté chorizo in an 8-inch nonstick omelet pan or skillet with sloped sides 7 to 10 minutes or until browned. Remove from skillet, and drain on paper towels. Wipe skillet clean.
2. Melt 1 Tbsp. butter in skillet, and sauté green onions, bell pepper, and jalapeño pepper over medium-high heat 3 to 5 minutes or until tender. Transfer to a bowl; stir in chorizo. Wipe skillet clean.
3. Whisk together cornmeal mix, buttermilk, milk, all-purpose flour, and 1 large egg.
4. Coat skillet with cooking spray; melt 1 Tbsp. butter in skillet over medium-high heat, rotating pan to coat bottom evenly. Pour about ⅓ cup cornmeal mixture into skillet. Tilt pan so uncooked portion flows around to coat bottom of pan, cooking until almost set, bubbles form, and edges are dry (about 1½ minutes). Gently flip with a spatula.
5. Sprinkle 1 side of omelet with about ½ cup onion mixture and about 3 Tbsp. cheese. Fold omelet in half; cook 30 seconds or until cheese is melted. Transfer to a serving plate; keep warm. Repeat procedure 4 times with remaining butter, cornmeal mixture, onion mixture, and cheese. Serve immediately.

A feather-light cornbread batter takes the place of eggs in these fun omelets.

Tomato-Herb Frittata

The secret to this recipe is an ovenproof nonstick pan, which allows the eggs to cook properly, keeps them from sticking, and simplifies cleanup.

MAKES 6 to 8 servings • **HANDS-ON TIME:** 27 min. • **TOTAL TIME:** 39 min.

- 2 Tbsp. olive oil
- 1 garlic clove, minced
- ½ (6-oz.) package fresh baby spinach
- 1 (10-oz.) can mild diced tomatoes and green chiles, drained (we tested with Rotel)
- ¼ tsp. salt
- ¼ tsp. pepper
- 12 large eggs, beaten*
- ½ cup crumbled garlic-and-herb feta cheese**

1. Preheat oven to 350°. Heat oil in a 10-inch (2-inch-deep) ovenproof nonstick skillet over medium-high heat.
2. Add garlic, and sauté 1 minute. Stir in spinach, and cook, stirring constantly, 1 minute or just until spinach begins to wilt.
3. Add tomatoes and green chiles, salt, and pepper, and cook, stirring frequently, 2 to 3 minutes or until spinach is wilted. Add eggs, and sprinkle with cheese. Cook 3 to 5 minutes, gently lifting edges of frittata with a spatula and tilting pan so uncooked portion flows underneath.
4. Bake at 350° for 12 to 15 minutes or until set and lightly browned. Remove from oven, and let stand 5 minutes. Slide frittata onto a large platter, and cut into 8 wedges.
*1 (32-oz.) carton egg substitute may be substituted. Increase bake time to 16 to 18 minutes or until set.
**Plain feta cheese may be substituted.

Tomato-Sausage Frittata: Brown ½ lb. ground pork sausage in a 10-inch (2-inch-deep) ovenproof nonstick skillet over medium-high heat, stirring often, 7 to 8 minutes or until sausage crumbles and is no longer pink; remove from skillet, and drain. Wipe skillet clean. Proceed with recipe as directed, adding sausage with tomatoes and green chiles in Step 3.

Bacon-Mushroom Frittata: Prepare recipe as directed in Step 1, sautéing ½ cup sliced fresh mushrooms in hot oil 2 to 3 minutes or until browned. Proceed with recipe as directed, stirring 3 cooked and chopped bacon slices in with tomatoes.

Eggplant-and-Olive Frittata: Prepare recipe as directed in Step 1, sautéing 1 cup peeled and chopped eggplant 5 minutes or until tender. Proceed with recipe as directed, stirring ½ cup sliced black olives in with tomatoes.

Sausage-and-Cheese Frittata

For an easy side, toss together fresh spinach leaves, sliced red onions, and toasted almonds with your favorite bottled vinaigrette.

kids' favorite

MAKES 6 servings • **HANDS-ON TIME:** 25 min. • **TOTAL TIME:** 48 min.

- 1 (12-oz.) package reduced-fat ground pork sausage
- 8 large eggs
- ⅓ cup milk
- ½ tsp. pepper
- ¼ tsp. salt
- 1 Tbsp. butter
- 1 cup (4 oz.) shredded 2% reduced-fat Cheddar cheese

1. Preheat oven to 350°. Brown sausage in a 10-inch ovenproof nonstick skillet over medium-high heat 10 minutes or until sausage crumbles and is no longer pink; drain and transfer to a bowl. Wipe skillet clean.
2. Whisk together eggs and next 3 ingredients until well blended.
3. Melt butter in skillet over medium heat; remove from heat, and pour half of egg mixture into skillet. Sprinkle with cooked sausage and cheese. Top with remaining egg mixture.
4. Bake at 350° for 23 to 25 minutes or until set.

Asparagus and Bacon Frittata

MAKES 8 servings • **HANDS-ON TIME:** 20 min. • **TOTAL TIME:** 45 min.

- 6 large plum tomatoes
- 1 (12-oz.) package bacon slices
- 1 medium onion, chopped
- 2 garlic cloves, pressed
- 2 cups (½-inch) pieces fresh asparagus
- 10 large eggs, lightly beaten
- ½ tsp. seasoned salt
- ¼ tsp. pepper
- ½ cup sour cream
- ¼ cup fresh parsley, chopped
- 2 cups (8 oz.) shredded mild Cheddar cheese, divided

1. Preheat oven to 350°. Cut tomatoes into thin slices. Drain tomatoes well, pressing between layers of paper towels to remove excess moisture; set aside.

2. Cook bacon in a 12-inch ovenproof skillet until crisp; remove bacon, reserving 1 Tbsp. drippings in skillet. Crumble bacon, and set aside.

3. Sauté onion and garlic in reserved hot drippings 4 to 5 minutes or until tender. Add asparagus, and sauté 1 minute.

4. Beat eggs, salt, and pepper at medium-high speed with an electric mixer until foamy; stir in sour cream. Pour over vegetables in skillet. Reserve ¼ cup bacon; stir in remaining bacon, parsley, and 1 cup cheese.

5. Cook over medium-low heat 3 to 4 minutes or until eggs begin to set around edges. Bake at 350° for 15 minutes. Remove from oven; top with tomato slices, reserved ¼ cup bacon, and remaining 1 cup cheese. Bake 10 to 15 more minutes or until frittata appears to be set.

Plum tomatoes, onion, and asparagus lend garden-fresh flavor to this Italian omelet.

Farmers Market Scramble

30-minute special

Fresh herbs and tomato give these eggs a punch of flavor.

MAKES 6 servings • **HANDS-ON TIME:** 24 min. • **TOTAL TIME:** 24 min.

- **12 large eggs**
- **¼ cup milk**
- **¼ cup whipping cream**
- **¾ tsp. salt**
- **¼ tsp. freshly ground pepper**
- **¼ tsp. hot sauce**
- **2 Tbsp. butter**
- **1 tomato, chopped and drained on a paper towel**
- **¼ cup chopped fresh chives**
- **2 Tbsp. chopped fresh flat-leaf parsley**

1. Whisk together first 6 ingredients in a large bowl until blended.
2. Melt 2 Tbsp. butter in a large nonstick skillet over medium heat. Add egg mixture; cook, without stirring, until eggs begin to set on bottom. Draw a spatula across bottom of skillet to form large curds. Cook until eggs are thickened but still moist. (Do not stir constantly.) Remove from heat, and transfer to a warm platter. Sprinkle eggs with tomato, chives, and parsley; serve hot.

How To Scramble Eggs

Take care not to stir the eggs too much while they cook. Simply draw a heat-resistant spatula through egg mixture as it begins to set on the bottom, forming large curds. Continue until eggs are thickened but still moist; do not stir constantly or they'll become dry and crumbly.

Ham-and-Cheese Croissant Casserole

You can substitute leftover baked ham for chopped ham in this dish. Nutmeg is optional, but adds a subtle touch of spice.

make ahead

MAKES 6 servings • **HANDS-ON TIME:** 15 min. • **TOTAL TIME:** 9 hr., 15 min.

- 3 (5-inch) large croissants
- 1 (8-oz.) package chopped cooked ham
- 1 (5-oz.) package shredded Swiss cheese
- 6 large eggs
- 1 cup half-and-half
- 1 Tbsp. dry mustard
- 2 Tbsp. honey
- ½ tsp. salt
- ½ tsp. pepper
- ¼ tsp. ground nutmeg (optional)

1. Cut croissants in half lengthwise, and cut each half into 4 to 5 pieces. Place croissant pieces in a lightly greased 10-inch deep-dish pie plate. Top with ham and cheese.

2. Whisk together eggs, next 5 ingredients, and, if desired, nutmeg in a large bowl.

3. Pour egg mixture over mixture in pie plate, pressing croissants down to submerge in egg mixture. Cover tightly, and chill 8 to 24 hours.

4. Preheat oven to 325°. Bake, covered, 35 minutes. Uncover and bake 25 to 30 more minutes or until browned and set. Let stand 10 minutes before serving.

Three-Cheese and Chile Casserole

Green chiles add a Western accent to this cheesy egg casserole.

MAKES 8 servings • **HANDS-ON TIME:** 8 min. • **TOTAL TIME:** 43 min.

- 8 large eggs, lightly beaten
- ½ cup all-purpose flour
- 1 tsp. baking powder
- 1 (16-oz.) container small-curd cottage cheese
- 2 cups (8 oz.) shredded Monterey Jack cheese
- 2 cups (8 oz.) shredded Cheddar cheese
- 2 (4.5-oz.) cans chopped green chiles
- ¼ cup butter, melted
- ½ tsp. garlic powder
- ½ tsp. chili powder

1. Preheat oven to 325°. Combine eggs, flour, and baking powder, stirring well. Stir in cheeses and remaining ingredients. Pour mixture into a lightly greased 13- x 9-inch baking dish.
2. Bake, uncovered, at 325° for 35 minutes.

SHORTCUT SECRET

If you need to serve a lot of eggs at one time, baking is a good choice. Eggs require little attention as they bake. Serve baked eggs immediately.

Greek Spinach Quiche

Feta and oregano give this quiche Grecian flair.

MAKES 8 servings • **HANDS-ON TIME:** 10 min. • **TOTAL TIME:** 1 hr., 3 min.

- ½ (14.1-oz.) package refrigerated piecrusts
- 3 large eggs, lightly beaten
- 1 cup milk
- ¼ cup butter, melted
- 2 Tbsp. all-purpose flour
- 2 Tbsp. grated Parmesan cheese
- ¼ tsp. salt
- ¼ tsp. dried oregano
- Dash of ground nutmeg
- 1 (10-oz.) package frozen chopped spinach, thawed and well drained
- 1 cup crumbled feta cheese

1. Preheat oven to 400°. Fit piecrust into a 9-inch pie plate according to package directions; fold edges under, and crimp. Prick bottom and sides of piecrust with a fork. Bake at 400° for 3 minutes; remove from oven, and gently prick with a fork. Bake 5 more minutes. Set aside.
2. Reduce oven temperature to 350°. Combine eggs and next 7 ingredients; stir with a wire whisk until blended. Stir in spinach and feta cheese; pour into piecrust. Bake at 350° for 35 minutes or until quiche is set and golden. Let stand 10 minutes.

Chiles Rellenos Quiche

All the cheesy goodness of the popular breakfast pie without the hassle of a crust.

MAKES 6 servings • **HANDS-ON TIME:** 12 min. • **TOTAL TIME:** 1 hr., 7 min.

- 2 (4-oz.) cans diced green chiles, drained
- 2 cups (8 oz.) shredded sharp Cheddar cheese
- 1 cup (4 oz.) shredded pepper Jack cheese
- 2 cups 2% reduced-fat milk
- 1 cup all-purpose baking mix
- 4 large eggs, lightly beaten
- 1 cup part-skim ricotta cheese

1. Preheat oven to 350°. Sprinkle green chiles, Cheddar cheese, and pepper Jack cheese into a lightly greased 11- x 8-inch baking dish.
2. Beat milk, baking mix, and eggs at low speed with an electric mixer until smooth. Stir in ricotta cheese; pour mixture evenly over chiles and cheeses in baking dish.
3. Bake, uncovered, at 350° for 45 minutes or until a knife inserted in center comes out clean. Let stand 10 minutes before cutting.

Chiles Rellenos Quiche

Ham-and-Bacon Quiche

MAKES 6 to 8 servings • **HANDS-ON TIME:** 20 min. • **TOTAL TIME:** 1 hr., 20 min.

- 1 (14.1-oz.) package refrigerated piecrusts
- 1 egg white, lightly beaten
- Parchment paper
- 6 bacon slices
- 1 cup sliced fresh mushrooms
- ½ cup chopped onion
- 1½ cups half-and-half
- 1 cup chopped cooked ham
- 6 large eggs, lightly beaten
- ½ tsp. seasoning salt
- ½ tsp. pepper
- 2 cups (8 oz.) shredded Swiss cheese
- 2 Tbsp. all-purpose flour

1. Preheat oven to 400°. Fit 1 piecrust into a 9-inch deep-dish pie plate according to package directions; trim dough around edges of pie plate.
2. Place remaining piecrust on a lightly floured surface; cut desired shapes with a decorative 1-inch cookie cutter. Brush edge of piecrust in pie plate with beaten egg white; gently press dough shapes onto edge of piecrust. Pierce bottom and sides with a fork.
3. Line piecrust with parchment paper or aluminum foil; fill piecrust with pie weights or dried beans.
4. Bake at 400° for 10 minutes. Remove weights and parchment paper; bake 5 more minutes, and set aside. Reduce oven temperature to 350°.
5. Cook bacon in a large skillet over medium-high heat until crisp. Remove bacon, and drain on paper towels, reserving 2 tsp. drippings in pan. Crumble bacon, and set aside.
6. Sauté mushrooms and chopped onion in hot drippings 3 to 4 minutes or until tender.
7. Stir bacon, half-and-half, and next 4 ingredients into onion mixture. Combine cheese and flour; add to bacon mixture, stirring until blended. Pour mixture into piecrust.
8. Bake at 350° for 45 to 50 minutes or until a wooden pick inserted in center comes out clean. (Shield edges with aluminum foil to prevent excess browning, if necessary.) Let stand 10 minutes before serving.

How To Dress It Up

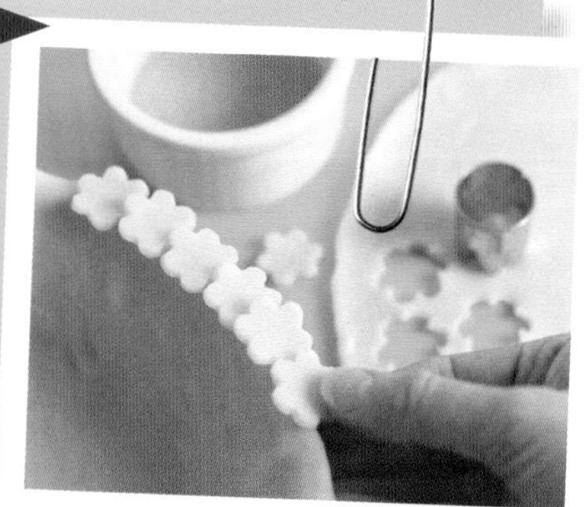

Use one refrigerated piecrust for the bottom of the quiche, and make it pretty with the second one. On a lightly floured surface, cut desired shapes from the piecrust using a decorative 1-inch cookie cutter. (Dress up any piecrust with this technique.) Brush edge of piecrust in pie plate with beaten egg white. Gently press cutouts onto edge of piecrust.

Crabmeat-Parmesan Quiche

A hint of lemon enhances the succulent, sweet goodness of crab.

MAKES 6 servings • **HANDS-ON TIME:** 15 min. • **TOTAL TIME:** 58 min.

- ½ (14.1-oz.) package refrigerated piecrusts
- 4 green onions, chopped
- 2 tsp. olive oil
- 1 lb. fresh lump crabmeat, drained
- 1 tsp. lemon zest
- ½ tsp. Old Bay seasoning
- ⅛ tsp. ground red pepper
- 1 cup half-and-half
- 3 large eggs
- ¼ tsp. salt
- ¼ tsp. black pepper
- 1 (5-oz.) package shredded Parmesan cheese

1. Preheat oven to 400°. Roll piecrust into a 13-inch circle on a flat surface. Fit into a 9-inch pie plate; fold edges under, and crimp. Bake on lowest oven rack at 400° for 8 minutes. Cool.
2. Sauté green onions in hot oil in a large skillet over medium-high heat 2 minutes. Stir in crabmeat and next 3 ingredients; sauté 2 minutes.
3. Whisk together half-and-half and next 3 ingredients in a large bowl; stir in cheese and crabmeat mixture. Pour filling into prepared crust.
4. Bake on lowest oven rack at 400° for 35 to 40 minutes or until set. Let stand 15 minutes before serving.

SHOPPER'S COMPANION

If you can't find fresh lump crabmeat, you can substitute 2 (6-oz.) cans lump crabmeat, drained and rinsed, for the fresh.

Over-the-Border Breakfast Sausage Wraps

MAKES 6 servings • **HANDS-ON TIME:** 33 min. • **TOTAL TIME:** 43 min.

- 1 (12-oz.) package 50%-less-fat ground pork sausage (we tested with Jimmy Dean)
- Vegetable cooking spray
- 1 to 2 tsp. hot sauce
- 1 (16-oz.) carton Southwestern-flavored egg substitute (we tested with Egg Beaters)
- 6 (8-inch) soft taco-size whole wheat or white flour tortillas
- 1½ cups (6 oz.) shredded reduced-fat Mexican cheese blend
- Toppings: salsa, nonfat sour cream, chopped green onions

1. Cook sausage in a large nonstick skillet coated with cooking spray over medium-high heat 10 minutes or until sausage crumbles and is no longer pink. Tilt pan to drain well; pat sausage dry with paper towels. Stir in hot sauce.

2. Cook egg substitute in a large skillet coated with cooking spray over medium-high heat, without stirring, 1 to 2 minutes or until mixture begins to set on bottom.

3. Gently stir to slightly break up eggs. Cook, stirring occasionally, 3 to 4 minutes or until eggs are thickened and moist. (Do not overstir.) Remove skillet from heat.

4. Lightly coat both sides of tortillas with cooking spray. Spoon sausage, eggs, and cheese down center of each tortilla. Fold sides over, enclosing filling completely, and gently press to seal.

5. Cook wraps, in 2 batches, folded sides down, in a large skillet coated with cooking spray over medium-high heat 3 minutes or until lightly browned. Carefully turn, and cook 2 to 3 more minutes or until lightly browned and cheese is melted. Cut each wrap in half, and serve immediately with desired toppings.

Anytime Tortillas

Wrap these individually in parchment paper or aluminum foil for a portable meal.

kids' favorite

MAKES 10 servings • **HANDS-ON TIME:** 28 min. • **TOTAL TIME:** 28 min.

- 10 (6-inch) fajita-size flour tortillas
- ½ (16-oz.) package ground pork sausage
- 6 large eggs
- Vegetable cooking spray
- ½ cup (2 oz.) shredded colby-Jack cheese blend
- Salsa (optional)
- Sour cream (optional)

1. Preheat oven to 250°. Wrap tortillas loosely with aluminum foil, and place in a 250° oven for 10 minutes.
2. Meanwhile, cook sausage in a large skillet over medium-high heat, stirring often, 8 minutes or until sausage crumbles and is no longer pink; drain, remove sausage from skillet, and pat dry with paper towels. Wipe skillet clean. Reduce heat to medium.
3. Whisk together eggs and 2 Tbsp. water. Coat same skillet with cooking spray; add egg mixture, and cook, without stirring, 2 to 3 minutes or until eggs begin to set on bottom. Gently draw cooked edges away from sides of pan to form large pieces. Cook, stirring occasionally, 2 minutes or until eggs are thickened but still moist. (Do not overstir.)
4. Spoon sausage and eggs evenly onto tortillas, and sprinkle with cheese; roll up tortillas. Serve with salsa and sour cream, if desired.

Breakfast Enchiladas

For make-ahead ease, prepare the recipe, without baking, and refrigerate overnight. Let stand at room temperature for 30 minutes; bake as directed.

MAKES 6 to 8 servings • **HANDS-ON TIME:** 20 min. • **TOTAL TIME:** 1 hr., 8 min., including sauce

- 1 (1-lb.) package hot ground pork sausage
- 2 Tbsp. butter
- 4 green onions, thinly sliced
- 2 Tbsp. chopped fresh cilantro
- 14 large eggs, beaten
- ¾ tsp. salt
- ½ tsp. pepper
- Cheese Sauce
- 8 (8-inch) flour tortillas
- 1 cup (4 oz.) shredded Monterey Jack cheese with jalapeños
- Toppings: halved grape tomatoes, sliced green onions, chopped fresh cilantro

1. Preheat oven to 350°. Cook sausage in a large nonstick skillet over medium-high heat, stirring until sausage crumbles and is no longer pink. Remove from pan; drain well, pressing between paper towels.
2. Melt butter in a large nonstick skillet over medium heat. Add green onions and 2 Tbsp. cilantro, and sauté 1 minute. Add eggs, salt, and pepper, and cook, without stirring, until eggs begin to set on bottom. Draw a spatula across bottom of pan to form large curds. Continue to cook until eggs are thickened but still moist; do not stir constantly. Remove from heat, and gently fold in 1½ cups Cheese Sauce and sausage.
3. Spoon about ⅓ cup egg mixture down center of each flour tortilla; roll up. Place, seam side down, in a lightly greased 13- x 9-inch baking dish. Pour remaining Cheese Sauce evenly over tortillas; sprinkle evenly with Monterey Jack cheese.
4. Bake at 350° for 30 minutes or until sauce is bubbly. Serve with desired toppings.

Cheese Sauce

MAKES about 4 cups • **HANDS-ON TIME:** 18 min. • **TOTAL TIME:** 18 min.

- ⅓ cup butter
- ⅓ cup all-purpose flour
- 3 cups milk
- 2 cups (8 oz.) shredded Cheddar cheese
- 1 (4.5-oz.) can chopped green chiles, undrained
- ¾ tsp. salt

1. Melt butter in a heavy saucepan over medium-low heat; whisk in flour until smooth. Cook, whisking constantly, 1 minute. Gradually whisk in milk; cook over medium heat, whisking constantly, 5 minutes or until thickened. Remove from heat, and whisk in remaining ingredients.

Sausage-and-Egg Casserole

An unbaked casserole can be covered with plastic wrap, then aluminum foil, and frozen up to 1 month. Thaw overnight in the refrigerator. Bake as directed.

MAKES 10 servings • **HANDS-ON TIME:** 20 min. • **TOTAL TIME:** 1 hr., 20 min.

make ahead

- **8 (1½-oz.) sourdough bread slices, cut into ½-inch cubes**
- **1 (12-oz.) package fully cooked pork sausage patties, chopped**
- **2½ cups 2% reduced-fat milk**
- **4 large eggs**
- **1 Tbsp. Dijon mustard**
- **½ cup buttermilk**
- **1 (10¾-oz.) can cream of mushroom soup**
- **1 cup (4 oz.) shredded sharp Cheddar cheese**

1. Preheat oven to 350°. Arrange bread in 2 lightly greased 8-inch square baking dishes or 1 lightly greased 13- x 9-inch baking dish. Top evenly with sausage. Whisk together 2½ cups milk, eggs, and Dijon mustard. Pour evenly over bread mixture.
2. Whisk together buttermilk and cream of mushroom soup. Spoon over bread mixture; sprinkle with Cheddar cheese. Place casserole on a baking sheet.
3. Bake at 350° for 1 hour or until casserole is set. Serve immediately.

You can use 1 (16-oz.) package of crumbled pork sausage cooked in a nonstick skillet until brown instead of the patties.

Breakfast Pizza

You can also bake this in a 12-inch deep-dish pizza pan or cake pan.

MAKES 8 servings • **HANDS-ON TIME:** 15 min. • **TOTAL TIME:** 50 min.

- **1 (8-oz.) can refrigerated crescent rolls**
- **1 lb. hot ground pork sausage**
- **1 (28-oz.) package frozen hash browns with onions and peppers**
- **1 cup (4 oz.) shredded Cheddar cheese**
- **4 large eggs**
- **½ cup milk**
- **1 tsp. salt**
- **½ tsp. pepper**

1. Preheat oven to 375°. Unroll crescent roll dough, and press on bottom and partially up sides of a 13- x 9-inch baking dish; press perforations to seal. Bake at 375° for 5 minutes.
2. Reduce oven temperature to 350°. Cook sausage in a large skillet over medium-high heat, stirring until sausage crumbles and is no longer pink. Drain well, and sprinkle evenly over crust.
3. Prepare frozen hash browns according to package directions, and spoon evenly over sausage. Sprinkle shredded cheese evenly over hash browns. (Cover and chill up to 24 hours, if desired.) Whisk together eggs and next 3 ingredients; pour evenly over cheese.
4. Bake at 350° for 30 to 35 minutes or until set.

Breakfast Pizza Cups

If you'd like to make this recipe more heart healthy, decrease the saturated fat and cholesterol by using egg substitute, lean ground turkey sausage, reduced-fat Cheddar cheese, and fat-free milk.

MAKES 12 servings • **HANDS-ON TIME:** 20 min. • **TOTAL TIME:** 38 min.

- ½ lb. bulk sausage
- 2 (13.8-oz.) cans refrigerated pizza crust dough
- ½ cup frozen hash browns, thawed
- ½ cup (2 oz.) shredded sharp Cheddar cheese
- 5 large eggs
- ½ cup milk
- ⅛ tsp. pepper
- 2 Tbsp. grated Parmesan cheese
- 1½ cups pizza sauce

1. Preheat oven to 375°. Cook sausage in a large skillet over medium-high heat 10 minutes or until sausage crumbles and is no longer pink. Drain well on paper towels, and set aside.
2. Roll or pat 1 can pizza crust dough into a 15- x 10-inch rectangle on a lightly floured surface; cut into 6 (5-inch) squares. Press squares into lightly greased muffin cups, skipping every other muffin cup. Repeat procedure with remaining can of pizza dough.
3. Spoon sausage evenly into crusts; sprinkle evenly with hash browns and Cheddar cheese.
4. Stir together eggs and next 2 ingredients; pour evenly into pizza cups, and sprinkle with grated Parmesan cheese.
5. Bake at 375° for 18 to 20 minutes or until golden. Serve with pizza sauce.

Guiltless French Toast

Guiltless French Toast

MAKES 4 servings • **HANDS-ON TIME:** 16 min. • **TOTAL TIME:** 16 min.

- 8 egg whites
- ¼ cup fresh orange juice
- 1 Tbsp. vanilla extract
- 1 tsp. ground cinnamon
- 4 whole grain bakery bread slices
- 1 Tbsp. butter
- ¼ cup maple syrup
- Fresh blueberries and kiwi slices

1. Whisk together first 4 ingredients in a shallow dish. Dip bread slices in egg mixture, coating both sides.

2. Melt butter on a griddle or in a large nonstick skillet over medium heat. Place bread slices on hot griddle, and pour remaining egg mixture over bread slices. Cook 3 to 4 minutes on each side or until golden. Drizzle with maple syrup, and top with fruit.

Oven-Baked French Toast

MAKES 8 servings • **HANDS-ON TIME:** 15 min. • **TOTAL TIME:** 9 hr.

- 1 (16-oz.) French bread loaf
- ¼ cup butter, softened
- 4 large eggs
- 1 cup milk
- ¼ cup sugar
- 2 Tbsp. maple syrup
- 1 tsp. vanilla extract
- ½ tsp. salt

1. Cut bread loaf into about 10 (¾-inch-thick) slices.

2. Spread butter evenly over 1 cut side of each bread slice.

3. Arrange bread, butter sides up, in an ungreased 13- x 9-inch baking dish.

4. Whisk together eggs and next 5 ingredients; pour over bread, pressing slices down. Cover and chill 8 hours.

5. Preheat oven to 350°. Remove bread slices from baking dish, and place on 2 lightly greased baking sheets. Bake, uncovered, at 350° for 45 minutes or until golden.

You can dust this French toast with powdered sugar just before serving.

pasta

Italian-Style Pizza Pot Pie

Discover an unexpected twist on a Southern favorite. This pot pie is topped with a package of refrigerated pizza crust dough to seal in the enticing flavor of meat-filled herbed tomato sauce.

kids' favorite

MAKES 4 to 6 servings • **HANDS-ON TIME:** 54 min. • **TOTAL TIME:** 1 hr., 15 min.

- ¾ **lb. ground round**
- ¼ **lb. mild Italian sausage, casings removed**
- 1 **small onion, chopped**
- 2 **garlic cloves, minced**
- 1 **(8-oz.) package sliced fresh mushrooms**
- 1 **(26-oz.) jar tomato-and-basil pasta sauce**
- ½ **tsp. dried Italian seasoning**
- ¼ **tsp. salt**
- 1 **(13.8-oz.) package refrigerated pizza crust dough (we tested with Pillsbury Classic Pizza Crust)**
- **Parchment paper**
- 1 **cup (4 oz.) shredded Italian five-cheese blend**

1. Preheat oven to 450°. Cook ground round and sausage in a large skillet over medium-high heat, stirring often, 8 to 10 minutes or until meat crumbles and is no longer pink. Drain beef mixture, reserving 1 tsp. drippings in skillet. Reduce heat to medium.

2. Sauté onion in hot drippings 2 minutes. Add garlic, and cook 1 minute or until tender. Add mushrooms, and sauté 8 to 10 minutes or until most of liquid has evaporated. Stir in beef mixture, pasta sauce, Italian seasoning, and salt. Bring to a light boil, and simmer 5 minutes.

3. Meanwhile, unroll dough on a lightly floured piece of parchment paper. Invert 1 (9-inch) round baking dish or pie plate onto center of dough. Cut dough around edge of baking dish, making a 9-inch circle. Remove excess dough around baking dish; cover and chill, reserving for another use. Remove baking dish.

4. Pour beef mixture into baking dish, and sprinkle with cheese. Immediately top with dough circle. Cut an "X" in top of dough for steam to escape. Place baking dish on an aluminum foil-lined baking sheet.

5. Bake at 450° for 16 to 20 minutes or until crust is golden brown. Let stand 10 minutes before serving.

Piecrust-Topped Pizza Pot Pie: Substitute ½ (14.1-oz.) package refrigerated piecrusts for pizza dough. Proceed with recipe as directed, omitting Step 3. (Place entire piecrust over filling in baking dish in Step 4; press crust onto edge of dish to secure. Edges of crust will hang over sides of dish. Tuck excess crust under sides of dish, if desired.)

Hawaiian Pizza

MAKES 4 servings • **HANDS-ON TIME:** 10 min. • **TOTAL TIME:** 50 min., including sauce

- ¾ cup Basic Tomato Sauce
- 2 (7-oz.) packages individual prebaked pizza crusts (we tested with Natural Gourmet Kabuli Pizza Crust)
- 1 cup diced smoked ham
- 1 cup chopped fresh pineapple
- ¼ cup diced green bell pepper
- ½ cup (2 oz.) shredded part-skim mozzarella cheese

1. Preheat oven to 450°. Spread 3 Tbsp. Basic Tomato Sauce over each of 4 individual pizza crusts. Top each with ¼ cup ham, ¼ cup chopped pineapple, and 1 Tbsp. diced bell pepper. Sprinkle each with 2 Tbsp. cheese. Bake at 450° on middle oven rack 10 to 12 minutes.

Basic Tomato Sauce

MAKES 2⅔ cups • **HANDS-ON TIME:** 30 min. • **TOTAL TIME:** 30 min.

- 4 to 5 garlic cloves, minced
- ½ tsp. dried crushed red pepper
- 2 Tbsp. extra virgin olive oil
- 1 (28-oz.) can crushed tomatoes
- ½ tsp. salt

1. Sauté garlic and crushed pepper in hot oil in a large saucepan over medium heat 1 minute. (Do not brown garlic.) Stir in tomatoes and salt. Bring sauce to a boil, reduce heat to low, and simmer, stirring occasionally, 15 minutes.

Use smaller prebaked crusts for individual pizzas or large rounds to serve a crowd.

Antipasto Pizza

Roasted or marinated vegetables, such as red bell peppers, assorted olives, or pickled okra, would also taste great on this zesty pie.

MAKES 4 servings • **HANDS-ON TIME:** 10 min. • **TOTAL TIME:** 24 min.

- **1 (12-inch) prebaked pizza crust**
- **¼ cup refrigerated pesto**
- **¾ cup chopped artichoke hearts**
- **½ cup diced salami or deli ham**
- **¼ cup sliced banana peppers**
- **¼ cup sliced black olives**
- **¼ cup sun-dried tomatoes in oil, drained and chopped**
- **1½ cups (6 oz.) shredded mozzarella cheese**

1. Preheat oven to 450°. Spread pizza crust evenly with ¼ cup pesto. Sprinkle evenly with remaining ingredients.
2. Bake at 450° for 12 to 14 minutes or until cheese is melted.

How To Freeze Pesto

If you have leftover pesto, just freeze it. Thanks to olive oil, pesto retains its bright color when frozen. Just drop a tablespoon of pesto into each section of an ice-cube tray and freeze. Transfer the frozen cubes to a zip-top plastic freezer bag. Before using it, let the pesto thaw for a few hours. Pesto will keep in the freezer for up to 3 months and in the refrigerator for up to 5 days.

Shrimp Alfredo Pizza

MAKES 4 to 6 servings • **HANDS-ON TIME:** 30 min. • **TOTAL TIME:** 47 min.

- 1 (1.6-oz.) package dry Alfredo sauce mix
- 1 lb. unpeeled, medium-size fresh shrimp
- 3 bacon slices
- 1 medium onion, thinly sliced
- 2 garlic cloves, minced
- 1 tsp. dried oregano
- ¼ tsp. pepper
- 1 (16-oz.) package prebaked Italian pizza crust (we tested with Boboli)
- ⅓ cup (1½ oz.) shredded Parmesan cheese
- 1 (8-oz.) package shredded mozzarella cheese
- 2 plum tomatoes, chopped
- 1 tsp. dried parsley

1. Preheat oven to 400°. Prepare Alfredo sauce according to package directions. Set aside.
2. Peel shrimp, and devein, if desired. Set aside.
3. Cook bacon in a nonstick skillet until crisp; remove bacon, reserving drippings in skillet. Drain bacon on paper towels; crumble and set aside.
4. Add onion and garlic to skillet, and sauté over medium-high heat 3 minutes or until tender. Add shrimp, and sauté 2 minutes. Stir in oregano and pepper. Remove from heat.
5. Place crust on a baking sheet; spread with Alfredo sauce. Sprinkle evenly with shrimp mixture, bacon, Parmesan cheese, and remaining ingredients.
6. Bake at 400° for 12 minutes or until cheese is melted. Let stand 5 minutes before serving.

Garden Eggplant Pizza

MAKES 6 servings • **HANDS-ON TIME:** 40 min. • **TOTAL TIME:** 50 min.

- 1 large eggplant, peeled
- 1 medium tomato
- 1 red bell pepper
- 1 onion
- 1 small zucchini
- 3 Tbsp. olive oil, divided
- 1 (16-oz.) package prebaked Italian pizza crust (we tested with Boboli)
- 2 cups (8 oz.) shredded mozzarella cheese
- ½ tsp. dried basil
- ½ tsp. dried oregano
- ½ tsp. dried thyme
- ¼ tsp. garlic powder
- ½ tsp. salt
- ¼ tsp. freshly ground black pepper

1. Preheat oven to 425°. Chop eggplant and next 4 ingredients coarsely; sauté in 1 tablespoon oil in a large skillet over medium-high heat 10 minutes or until tender.
2. Layer pizza crust evenly with cheese and eggplant mixture; sprinkle with basil and next 5 ingredients. Drizzle with remaining 2 tablespoons oil.
3. Bake at 425° for 10 minutes or until golden.

To substitute fresh herbs, use 3 times more than dried.

Grilled Tomato-Peach Pizza

MAKES 6 servings • **HANDS-ON TIME:** 33 min. • **TOTAL TIME:** 48 min.

- Vegetable cooking spray
- 2 tomatoes, sliced
- ½ tsp. salt
- 1 large peach, peeled and sliced
- 1 lb. bakery pizza dough
- ½ (16-oz.) package fresh mozzarella cheese, sliced
- 4 to 6 fresh basil leaves
- Garnishes: coarsely ground pepper, olive oil

1. Coat cold cooking grate of grill with cooking spray, and place on grill. Preheat grill to 300° to 350° (medium) heat.
2. Sprinkle tomatoes with salt; let stand 15 minutes. Pat tomatoes dry with paper towels.
3. Grill peach slices, covered with grill lid, 2 to 3 minutes on each side or until grill marks appear.
4. Place dough on a large baking sheet coated with cooking spray; lightly coat dough with cooking spray. Roll dough to ¼-inch thickness (about 14 inches in diameter). Slide pizza dough from baking sheet onto cooking grate.
5. Grill, covered with grill lid, 2 to 3 minutes or until lightly browned. Turn dough over, and reduce temperature to 250° to 300° (low) heat; top with tomatoes, grilled peaches, and mozzarella. Grill, covered with grill lid, 5 more minutes or until cheese melts. Arrange basil leaves over pizza. Serve immediately. Garnish, if desired.

Pizza with Tomatoes, Asparagus, and Basil

MAKES 4 servings • **HANDS-ON TIME:** 10 min. • **TOTAL TIME:** 25 min.

- 1 cup (1½-inch) diagonally cut asparagus (about ½ lb.)
- 1 (10-oz.) thin Italian cheese-flavored pizza crust (we tested with Boboli)
- Vegetable cooking spray
- 2 Tbsp. commercial pesto (we tested with Classico)
- 6 plum tomatoes, cut into ¼-inch-thick slices (about ¾ lb.)
- 1 cup (4 oz.) shredded part-skim mozzarella cheese
- ¼ cup thinly sliced fresh basil

1. Preheat oven to 450°.
2. Steam asparagus, covered, 2 minutes or until crisp-tender. Rinse under cold running water; drain well, and pat dry with paper towels.
3. Place pizza crust on an ungreased pizza pan or baking sheet. Lightly coat pizza crust with cooking spray. Spread pesto evenly over crust. Arrange tomatoes and asparagus over pesto. Sprinkle with cheese. Bake at 450° for 15 minutes or until cheese melts and pizza is thoroughly heated. Remove from oven, and sprinkle with basil.
4. Cut into 8 slices, and serve immediately.

Roasted Vegetable-and-Goat Cheese Pizza

You can use more or less cheese depending on what you have available; substituting 2 (4-oz.) logs or most of an 11-oz. log works just fine.

MAKES 2 (12-inch) pizzas • **HANDS-ON TIME:** 30 min. • **TOTAL TIME:** 1 hr., 45 min.

- **1 medium-size sweet onion, cut into ¾-inch pieces**
- **1 tsp. olive oil**
- **1 medium eggplant, peeled and cut into ¾-inch cubes**
- **1 red bell pepper, cut into ¾-inch pieces**
- **1 small zucchini, cut into ¾-inch cubes**
- **1 Tbsp. olive oil**
- **2 tsp. chopped fresh thyme**
- **1 tsp. salt**
- **½ tsp. pepper**
- **1 (24-oz.) package prebaked pizza crusts**
- **1 (7-oz.) container refrigerated prepared pesto sauce**
- **1 (9-oz.) package goat cheese, crumbled**
- **¼ cup pine nuts**

1. Preheat oven to 425°. Toss onion with 1 tsp. oil; arrange on an aluminum foil-lined jelly-roll or broiler pan.
2. Bake at 425° for 20 minutes or until tender, stirring after 10 minutes.
3. Toss together eggplant and next 6 ingredients; add to onion on jelly-roll pan. Bake 30 more minutes, stirring at 10-minute intervals.
4. Place pizza crusts on 2 lightly greased baking sheets; spread pesto evenly over crusts, and arrange vegetables evenly over pesto. Sprinkle crumbled goat cheese and ¼ cup pine nuts over vegetables.
5. Bake pizzas at 425° for 25 minutes or until cheese is lightly browned.

Grilled Heirloom Tomato and Goat Cheese Pizza

MAKES 6 servings • **HANDS-ON TIME:** 15 min. • **TOTAL TIME:** 15 min.

- 1 (13.8-oz.) can refrigerated pizza crust dough
- Vegetable cooking spray
- 1 garlic clove, halved
- 1 large heirloom tomato, seeded and chopped (about 10 oz.)
- ½ cup (2 oz.) shredded part-skim mozzarella cheese
- ¾ cup (3 oz.) crumbled herbed goat cheese

1. Preheat grill to 300° to 350° (medium) heat.
2. Unroll dough onto a large baking sheet coated with cooking spray; pat dough into a 12- x 9-inch rectangle. Lightly coat dough with cooking spray.
3. Place dough on grill rack coated with cooking spray; grill 1 minute or until lightly browned. Turn crust over. Rub with garlic; sprinkle with tomato and cheeses. Close grill lid; grill 3 minutes. Serve immediately.

SHOPPER'S COMPANION

Heirloom tomatoes are remarkably flavorful and colorful compared to their grocery store counterparts. They vary from red to orange, gold, taxi yellow, nearly white, pink, purplish black, and green. Some are even multicolored, such as Mr. Stripey. Your choice of tomato will shine in this simple pizza.

Portobello Pizza

Baking the crust on the bottom rack will keep it from becoming soggy.

MAKES 6 servings • **HANDS-ON TIME:** 15 min. • **TOTAL TIME:** 38 min.

- 2 large portobello mushroom caps, sliced*
- ½ large onion, sliced
- ½ tsp. salt
- ½ tsp. pepper
- Vegetable cooking spray
- 1 Tbsp. balsamic vinegar
- 2 Tbsp. yellow cornmeal
- 1 (13.8-oz.) refrigerated pizza crust dough
- 2 Tbsp. basil pesto
- 2 Tbsp. plain nonfat yogurt
- ¼ cup chopped fresh basil
- 6 fresh mozzarella cheese slices (6 oz.)**
- 5 plum tomatoes, chopped
- 2 Tbsp. shredded Parmesan cheese

1. Preheat oven to 425°. Sauté first 4 ingredients in a large skillet coated with cooking spray over medium-high heat 5 minutes or until onion is tender. Add balsamic vinegar; cook 2 minutes or until liquid is evaporated. Set aside.

2. Sprinkle cornmeal over baking pan; spread out pizza dough. Bake at 425° on bottom oven rack 5 minutes.

3. Stir together pesto and yogurt. Spread over pizza crust, leaving a 1-inch border. Sprinkle pizza with mushroom mixture and fresh basil. Top with mozzarella cheese and tomatoes. Sprinkle with Parmesan cheese.

4. Bake at 425° on bottom oven rack 18 more minutes or until edges are golden brown and cheese is melted.

***1** (8-oz.) package sliced button mushrooms may be substituted for the portobello mushroom caps.

****1½** cups (6 oz.) shredded part-skim mozzarella cheese may be substituted for fresh mozzarella.

SHOPPER'S COMPANION

Let a crimini mushroom grow a few days longer, and you end up with a portobello. This flying saucer-shaped mushroom, which often measures from 3 to 6 inches across, is firm, meaty, and intensely flavorful.

Chicken Sausage, Sweet Onion, and Fennel Pizza

MAKES 4 servings • **HANDS-ON TIME:** 20 min. • **TOTAL TIME:** 32 min.

- 3 oz. chicken apple sausage, chopped (we tested with Gerhard's)
- 2 tsp. olive oil
- 1½ cups vertically sliced Oso Sweet or other sweet onion
- 1 cup thinly sliced fennel bulb (about 1 small bulb)
- ¼ tsp. salt
- 1 (12-oz.) prebaked pizza crust (we tested with Mama Mary's)
- ¾ cup (3 oz.) shredded Gouda cheese
- 1 Tbsp. chopped fresh chives

1. Preheat oven to 450°.
2. Heat a large nonstick skillet over medium-high heat. Add sausage to pan; sauté 4 minutes or until browned, stirring occasionally. Remove from pan.
3. Add oil to pan. Add onion, fennel, and salt; cover and cook 10 minutes or until tender and lightly browned, stirring occasionally.
4. Place pizza crust on a baking sheet. Top evenly with onion mixture; sprinkle with cheese, and top evenly with sausage. Bake at 450° for 12 minutes or until cheese melts. Sprinkle evenly with chives. Cut pizza into 8 wedges.

Quick 'n' Easy Chicken Barbecue Pizza

company's coming

MAKES 6 servings • **HANDS-ON TIME:** 24 min. • **TOTAL TIME:** 44 min.

- 1 small onion, chopped
- ½ red bell pepper, chopped
- ½ tsp. salt
- ¼ tsp. pepper
- 1 tsp. olive oil
- 1 (10-oz.) can refrigerated pizza crust
- ½ cup hickory smoke barbecue sauce
- 2 (6-oz.) packages grilled boneless, skinless chicken breast strips
- 2 cups (8 oz.) shredded Monterey Jack cheese with peppers
- Garnish: chopped fresh parsley
- Hickory smoke barbecue sauce

1. Preheat oven to 400°. Sauté first 4 ingredients in hot oil in a large skillet over medium-high heat 8 to 10 minutes or until vegetables are tender. Drain well.
2. Unroll pizza crust; press or pat into a lightly greased 13- x 9-inch pan.
3. Bake crust at 400° for 12 to 14 minutes. Spread ½ cup barbecue sauce evenly over top of pizza crust in pan. Arrange chicken strips evenly over barbecue sauce, top with onion mixture, and sprinkle evenly with cheese.
4. Bake at 400° for 8 to 10 minutes or until cheese melts. Garnish, if desired. Serve with extra sauce for dipping.

Quick 'n' Easy Chicken Barbecue Pizza

Chicken Parmesan Pizza

For an easy side, toss together romaine lettuce, cracked pepper, and grated Parmesan cheese; toss with your favorite bottled Caesar dressing. Sprinkle with croutons.

kids' favorite

MAKES 4 servings • **HANDS-ON TIME:** 14 min. • **TOTAL TIME:** 30 min.

- 1 (10-oz.) package frozen garlic bread loaf
- ½ cup canned pizza sauce
- 6 deli fried chicken strips
- 1 cup (4 oz.) shredded Italian three-cheese blend
- 2 Tbsp. chopped fresh basil

1. Preheat oven to 400°. Arrange garlic bread, buttered sides up, on a baking sheet.
2. Bake at 400° for 8 to 9 minutes or until bread is lightly browned. Spread pizza sauce over garlic bread.
3. Cut chicken strips into ½-inch pieces, and arrange over pizza sauce. Sprinkle with cheese and basil.
4. Bake at 400° for 8 to 10 minutes or until cheese melts. Serve immediately.

Sausage Italian Bread Pizza

Choose your favorite sauce for this quick pizza. Most supermarkets have a good selection of jarred pasta and pizza sauces ranging in flavor from simple marinara to roasted bell pepper.

kids' favorite

MAKES 4 servings • **HANDS-ON TIME:** 30 min. • **TOTAL TIME:** 38 min.

- 1 lb. mild or hot Italian sausage
- 2 Tbsp. olive oil, divided
- 1 onion, halved and thinly sliced
- 2 garlic cloves, minced
- 1 cup pizza or pasta sauce
- 1½ tsp. dried oregano
- ¼ tsp. dried crushed red pepper
- ¼ tsp. salt
- 1 (1-lb.) loaf semolina bread (about 14 inches long)
- ⅔ cup ricotta cheese
- 2 cups (8 oz.) shredded mozzarella cheese
- ¼ cup grated Parmesan cheese

1. Preheat oven to 425°. Remove and discard casings from sausage. Cook sausage in a large skillet over medium-high heat 8 minutes, stirring until meat crumbles and is no longer pink. Push meat to outer edges of pan; add 1 Tbsp. oil. Add onion and garlic; cook 5 minutes or until onion is softened. Remove from heat; stir in pizza sauce and next 3 ingredients.
2. Cut bread in half lengthwise using a serrated knife, and scoop out center of each bread half, leaving a ½-inch border; discard scooped-out bread or reserve for making breadcrumbs.
3. Spread ⅓ cup ricotta down center of each bread half. Top each evenly with sausage mixture, mozzarella, and Parmesan cheese. Drizzle pizzas evenly with remaining 1 Tbsp. oil. Place pizzas on a lightly greased baking sheet.
4. Bake at 425° for 6 minutes or until cheese is melted and pizzas are thoroughly heated.

Baked Linguine with Meat Sauce

MAKES 8 servings • **HANDS-ON TIME:** 40 min. • **TOTAL TIME:** 1 hr., 15 min.

2 lb. lean ground beef
2 garlic cloves, minced
1 (28-oz.) can crushed tomatoes
1 (8-oz.) can tomato sauce
1 (6-oz.) can tomato paste
2 tsp. sugar
1 tsp. salt
8 oz. uncooked linguine
1 (16-oz.) container sour cream
1 (8-oz.) package cream cheese, softened
1 bunch green onions, chopped
2 cups (8 oz.) shredded sharp Cheddar cheese

1. Preheat oven to 350°. Cook beef and garlic in a Dutch oven, stirring until beef crumbles and is no longer pink. Stir in tomatoes and next 4 ingredients; simmer 30 minutes. Set mixture aside.
2. Cook pasta according to package directions; drain. Place in a lightly greased 13- x 9-inch baking dish.
3. Stir together sour cream, cream cheese, and green onions. Spread over pasta. Top with meat sauce.
4. Bake at 350° for 20 to 25 minutes or until thoroughly heated. Sprinkle with Cheddar cheese, and bake 5 more minutes or until cheese melts. Let stand 5 minutes. Serve with a salad and bread, if desired.

How To Brown Ground Beef

Don't add meat to a cold pan. Heat the pan until it's hot before adding the meat. And don't overcrowd your pan.

Saucy Manicotti

Crusty cheese bubbling over gratin dishes and hiding a thick meat sauce will please anyone at your dinner table.

company's coming

MAKES 7 servings • **HANDS-ON TIME:** 40 min. • **TOTAL TIME:** 1 hr., 30 min.

- **1 (8-oz.) package manicotti shells**
- **1 (16-oz.) package Italian sausage, casings removed**
- **1 large onion, chopped**
- **9 garlic cloves, pressed**
- **1 (26-oz.) jar seven-herb tomato pasta sauce**
- **6 cups (24 oz.) shredded mozzarella cheese, divided**
- **1 (15-oz.) container ricotta cheese**
- **1 (8-oz.) container chive-and-onion cream cheese**
- **¾ cup freshly grated Parmesan cheese**
- **¾ tsp. freshly ground pepper**

1. Cook manicotti shells according to package directions.
2. Cook sausage, onion, and half of pressed garlic in a large Dutch oven over medium-high heat 6 minutes, stirring until sausage crumbles and is no longer pink. Stir in pasta sauce; bring to a boil. Remove from heat.
3. Preheat oven to 350°. Combine 4 cups mozzarella cheese, next 4 ingredients, and remaining pressed garlic in a large bowl, stirring until blended. Cut a slit down length of each cooked manicotti shell.
4. Spoon ¼ cup sauce into each of 7 lightly greased 8-oz. shallow baking dishes. Spoon cheese mixture into manicotti shells, gently pressing cut sides together. Arrange stuffed shells over sauce in dishes, seam sides down. Spoon remaining sauce (about ¾ cup per dish) over stuffed shells. Sprinkle with remaining 2 cups mozzarella cheese.
5. Bake, uncovered, at 350° for 50 minutes.

SHORTCUT SECRET

To bake in a single casserole dish, spoon 1 cup sauce into a lightly greased 13-x 9-inch baking dish. Arrange stuffed shells over sauce in dish. Top with remaining sauce and remaining mozzarella cheese. Bake, uncovered, at 350° for 50 minutes or until bubbly.

Pronto Stuffed Pasta Shells

We used half of one of the Herb-Roasted Chickens in this recipe. To cut the cook time almost in half, start with 2 cups chopped chicken from a rotisserie chicken.

MAKES 4 to 6 servings • **HANDS-ON TIME:** 35 min. • **TOTAL TIME:** 3 hr., 25 min., including chickens

- **18 jumbo pasta shells**
- **2 (10-oz.) packages frozen chopped spinach, thawed**
- **2 cups chopped cooked Herb-Roasted Chickens**
- **1 (16-oz.) container low-fat cottage cheese**
- **¼ cup grated Parmesan cheese**
- **1 large egg, lightly beaten**
- **1 Tbsp. chopped fresh basil**
- **¼ tsp. ground nutmeg**
- **1 (16-oz.) jar Alfredo sauce**

1. Preheat oven to 350°. Prepare pasta shells according to package directions.
2. Meanwhile, drain chopped spinach well, pressing between paper towels.
3. Stir together spinach, chicken, and next 5 ingredients. Spoon mixture evenly into shells.
4. Spread half of jarred Alfredo sauce in a lightly greased 13- x 9-inch baking dish. Arrange stuffed pasta shells over sauce, and pour remaining sauce over shells.
5. Bake, covered, at 350° for 40 to 45 minutes or until filling is hot and sauce is bubbly. Remove from oven, and let stand 10 minutes.

Herb-Roasted Chickens

MAKES 8 to 12 servings • **HANDS-ON TIME:** 20 min. • **TOTAL TIME:** 2 hr.

- **6 Tbsp. olive oil**
- **½ cup poultry seasoning**
- **¼ cup fresh rosemary leaves, finely chopped**
- **¼ cup fresh thyme leaves, finely chopped**
- **4 tsp. fresh minced garlic**
- **2 tsp. salt**
- **1 tsp. pepper**
- **2 (3- to 4-lb.) whole chickens**

1. Preheat oven to 425°. Stir together oil and next 6 ingredients until well blended.
2. If necessary, remove giblets and neck from chickens, and reserve for another use. Rinse chickens with cold water; pat dry.
3. Loosen and lift skin from chicken breasts with fingers (do not totally detach skin). Rub 2 Tbsp. olive oil mixture evenly underneath skin of each chicken. Carefully replace skin. Rub remaining olive oil mixture over both chickens, coating evenly. Place chickens, side by side, on a lightly greased wire rack in a pan.
4. Bake at 425° for 30 minutes; cover loosely with aluminum foil, and bake 45 to 55 more minutes or until a meat thermometer inserted in thickest portion of breast registers 165°. Let stand 15 minutes before slicing.

Cheese Ravioli with Spicy Tomato Sauce

MAKES 4 servings • **HANDS-ON TIME:** 30 min. • **TOTAL TIME:** 41 min.

- **1 cup ricotta cheese**
- **½ cup (2 oz.) freshly shredded Parmesan cheese**
- **¾ tsp. black pepper**
- **⅓ cup chopped fresh basil, divided**
- **½ (16-oz.) package won ton wrappers**
- **1 pt. cherry tomatoes, halved**
- **2 Tbsp. olive oil**
- **½ cup chicken broth**
- **1 tsp. white wine vinegar**
- **¼ to ½ tsp. dried crushed red pepper**
- **¼ tsp. salt**
- **Garnishes: fresh basil leaves, freshly shaved Parmesan cheese**

1. Stir together first 3 ingredients and 3 Tbsp. chopped fresh basil in a small bowl.

2. Arrange 1 won ton wrapper on a clean, flat surface. (Cover remaining wrappers with plastic wrap or a damp towel to prevent drying out.) Lightly moisten edges of wrapper with water. Place about 1½ tsp. cheese mixture in center of wrapper; fold 2 opposite corners together over cheese mixture, forming a triangle. Press edges together to seal, removing any air pockets. Cover with plastic wrap or a damp cloth. Repeat procedure with remaining wrappers and cheese mixture.

3. Cook ravioli, in 2 batches, in boiling salted water to cover in a Dutch oven over medium-high heat 3 minutes. Remove with a slotted spoon, and drain well on a lightly greased wire rack. Divide cooked ravioli among 4 individual serving bowls.

4. Sauté tomatoes in hot oil in a large skillet over medium-high heat 2 minutes or just until soft. Add broth and white wine vinegar; cook 2 to 3 minutes or until tomatoes begin to wilt. Stir in dried crushed red pepper, salt, and remaining chopped basil. Pour sauce over ravioli. Garnish, if desired. Serve immediately.

Bow-Tie Pasta Toss

MAKES 2 to 3 servings • **HANDS-ON TIME:** 15 min. • **TOTAL TIME:** 35 min.

- 8 oz. uncooked bow-tie pasta
- ¾ tsp. salt, divided
- 1 cup grape tomatoes, cut in half
- 1 (2.25-oz.) can sliced black olives, drained
- 1 Tbsp. finely chopped sweet onion
- 3 Tbsp. olive oil
- 3 Tbsp. balsamic vinegar
- 1 small garlic clove, pressed
- 1 tsp. chopped fresh oregano
- ½ (4-oz.) package crumbled feta cheese

Garnish: fresh oregano sprigs

1. Prepare pasta according to package directions, adding ½ tsp. salt to water; drain well.
2. Place pasta in a large bowl, and stir in tomatoes, olives, and onion.
3. Whisk together olive oil, next 3 ingredients, and remaining ¼ tsp. salt; add to pasta mixture, tossing to coat. Let stand 10 minutes; stir in feta. Garnish, if desired.

Bacon Bow-Tie Pasta

Bacon Bow-Tie Pasta

Pasta needs plenty of room to roam in rapidly boiling salted water. Using plenty of water and stirring 2 or 3 times during cooking keeps pasta from sticking or clumping.

MAKES 4 servings • **HANDS-ON TIME:** 25 min. • **TOTAL TIME:** 35 min.

- **½ (16-oz.) package farfalle (bow-tie) pasta**
- **½ lb. bacon**
- **1 (8-oz.) package cream cheese, softened**
- **¼ cup butter, softened**
- **1½ tsp. dried Italian seasoning**
- **⅔ cup milk**
- **½ cup grated Parmesan cheese**

1. Cook pasta according to package directions. Keep warm.
2. Cook bacon according to package directions; drain well, and crumble.
3. Beat cream cheese, butter, and Italian seasoning in a medium-size microwave-safe bowl at low speed with an electric mixer until smooth. Gradually add milk, beating until mixture is smooth.
4. Microwave cream cheese mixture at HIGH 3 minutes or until thoroughly heated, whisking every 30 seconds. Pour cream cheese mixture over warm pasta, tossing to coat. Top with ½ cup grated Parmesan cheese and crumbled bacon.

Lightened Bacon Bow-Tie Pasta: Substitute reduced-fat or turkey bacon, ⅓-less-fat cream cheese, and 2% reduced-fat milk. Proceed as directed.

Chicken and Bow-Tie Pasta

MAKES 4 servings • **HANDS-ON TIME:** 28 min. • **TOTAL TIME:** 40 min.

- **4 skinned and boned chicken breasts, cut into bite-size pieces**
- **8 oz. uncooked farfalle (bow-tie) pasta**
- **1 cup chicken broth**
- **1 celery rib, chopped (about ½ cup)**
- **1 small onion, chopped (about ½ cup)**
- **1 (10¾-oz.) can cream of mushroom soup**
- **1 (8-oz.) package pasteurized prepared cheese product, cubed**

Garnish: chopped fresh parsley

1. Bring 1 qt. salted water to a boil in a Dutch oven. Add chicken, and cook 12 minutes or until done. Remove chicken from water with a slotted spoon. Add pasta to water in Dutch oven, and cook 10 minutes or until tender; drain. Keep warm.
2. Heat ¼ cup broth over medium-high heat in a Dutch oven; add celery and onion, and cook 5 minutes or until tender. Stir in chicken, soup, cheese, and remaining ¾ cup chicken broth, stirring until cheese is melted. Toss with pasta; garnish, if desired. Serve immediately.

Cajun Chicken Pasta

MAKES 4 servings • **HANDS-ON TIME:** 25 min. • **TOTAL TIME:** 35 min.

- 12 oz. uncooked linguine
- 2 lb. chicken breast strips
- 1 Tbsp. Cajun seasoning
- 1¼ tsp. salt, divided
- ¼ cup butter
- 1 small red bell pepper, thinly sliced*
- 1 small green bell pepper, thinly sliced*
- 1 (8-oz.) package fresh mushrooms
- 2 green onions (white and light green parts only), sliced*
- 1½ cups half-and-half
- ¼ tsp. lemon pepper
- ¼ tsp. dried basil
- ¼ tsp. garlic powder

Garnish: chopped green onions

1. Prepare pasta according to package directions.
2. Sprinkle chicken evenly with Cajun seasoning and 1 tsp. salt. Melt ¼ cup butter in a large nonstick skillet over medium-high heat; add chicken, and sauté 5 to 6 minutes or until done. Remove chicken.
3. Add bell peppers, mushrooms, and green onions to skillet, and sauté 9 to 10 minutes or until vegetables are tender and liquid evaporates.
4. Return chicken to skillet; stir in half-and-half, next 3 ingredients, and remaining ¼ tsp. salt. Cook, stirring often, over medium-low heat 3 to 4 minutes or until thoroughly heated. Add linguine; toss to coat. Garnish, if desired, and serve immediately.
*½ (16-oz.) bag frozen sliced green, red, and yellow bell peppers and onion may be substituted. We tested with Birds Eye Pepper Stir-Fry.

SHOPPER'S COMPANION

To save time, substitute frozen peppers and onions (see directions at the end of recipe). Frozen vegetables are one of our favorite time-saving shortcuts. Neatly trimmed and perfectly chopped, they offer consistent quality year-round. Processed soon after harvest, frozen vegetables often exceed the nutritional value of fresh.

Asian Shrimp with Pasta

Asian Shrimp with Pasta

It may seem like a lot of ingredients, but you'll make this often, so keep these items on hand.

MAKES 6 servings • **HANDS-ON TIME:** 25 min. • **TOTAL TIME:** 33 min.

- **1 lb. unpeeled, medium-size shrimp**
- **1 (9-oz.) package refrigerated angel hair pasta**
- **¼ cup lite soy sauce**
- **¼ cup seasoned rice wine vinegar**
- **2 tsp. dark sesame oil**
- **6 green onions, chopped**
- **1 cup frozen sweet green peas, thawed**
- **1 (8-oz.) can sliced water chestnuts, drained**
- **¾ cup shredded carrots**
- **¼ cup chopped fresh cilantro**
- **2 Tbsp. minced fresh ginger**
- **2 garlic cloves, minced**
- **1 tsp. vegetable oil**
- **2 Tbsp. fresh lime juice**
- **½ tsp. freshly ground pepper**
- **2 Tbsp. chopped unsalted dry-roasted peanuts**

1. Peel shrimp, and devein, if desired. Set shrimp aside.
2. Prepare pasta according to package directions, omitting salt and fat. Drain and place in a large bowl or on a platter.
3. Stir together soy sauce, vinegar, and sesame oil. Drizzle over pasta. Add green onions and next 4 ingredients to pasta; toss.
4. Sauté ginger and garlic in hot vegetable oil 1 to 2 minutes. (Do not brown.) Add shrimp, lime juice, and pepper; cook 3 to 5 minutes or just until shrimp turn pink. Add shrimp mixture to pasta mixture, and toss. Sprinkle with peanuts. Serve immediately.

Noodle Bowl

You can substitute ½ cup chopped cooked chicken for the shrimp.

MAKES 1 serving • **HANDS-ON TIME:** 10 min. • **TOTAL TIME:** 15 min.

- **1 (3-oz.) package Oriental-flavored ramen noodle soup mix**
- **2 cups water**
- **1 chopped green onion**
- **2 Tbsp. chopped fresh cilantro**
- **½ cup fresh snow peas, trimmed**
- **6 peeled and deveined medium-size raw shrimp**
- **¼ cup shredded napa cabbage**
- **1 to 2 Tbsp. chopped peanuts**

1. Stir together flavor packet from ramen noodle soup mix, 2 cups water, chopped green onions, and chopped fresh cilantro in a medium saucepan. Bring to a boil; add noodles and snow peas. Cook 1 minute, and stir in shrimp. Cook 2 minutes. Transfer to a bowl, and top with shredded cabbage and chopped peanuts.

Shrimp Scampi

MAKES 4 servings • **HANDS-ON TIME:** 20 min. • **TOTAL TIME:** 30 min.

- **1 lb. peeled, large raw shrimp**
- **1 (12-oz.) package angel hair pasta**
- **½ cup butter**
- **¼ cup finely chopped onion**
- **3 garlic cloves, finely chopped**
- **1 tsp. salt-free Italian-herb seasoning (we tested with Mrs. Dash)**
- **1 tsp. Worcestershire sauce**
- **1 Tbsp. fresh lemon juice**
- **¼ cup freshly grated Romano or Parmesan cheese**
- **1 Tbsp. chopped fresh parsley**

1. Devein shrimp, if desired.
2. Prepare angel hair pasta according to package directions.
3. Meanwhile, melt butter in a large skillet over medium-high heat; add onion and garlic, and sauté 3 to 5 minutes or until tender. Stir in Italian-herb seasoning and Worcestershire sauce.
4. Reduce heat to medium. Add shrimp, and cook, stirring occasionally, 3 to 5 minutes or just until shrimp turn pink. Stir in lemon juice. Toss shrimp mixture with pasta, and sprinkle with cheese and parsley. Serve immediately.

Sautéed Shrimp and Pasta

Put the pasta on to cook as you start the shrimp to have dinner on the table in record time.

MAKES 4 servings • **HANDS-ON TIME:** 20 min. • **TOTAL TIME:** 20 min.

30-minute special

- ¼ cup butter
- 1 (0.7-oz.) envelope Italian dressing mix
- 1 lb. peeled and deveined medium-size raw shrimp
- 1 (9-oz.) package refrigerated fettuccine

1. Melt butter in a large skillet over medium heat; stir in dressing mix. Add shrimp; cook, stirring constantly, 3 to 5 minutes or until shrimp turn pink. Cook pasta according to package directions. Serve shrimp immediately over pasta.

How To Peel and Devein Shrimp

It's fastest to purchase shrimp that has already been peeled and deveined. But if you'd like to start with shrimp in the shell, begin by peeling the shrimp. Then cut a shallow slit along the back of the shrimp using a sharp paring knife. Lift and remove the dark vein with the knife tip. Rinse shrimp under cold water; drain. One lb. of shrimp in the shell equals ¾ lb. of peeled and deveined shrimp.

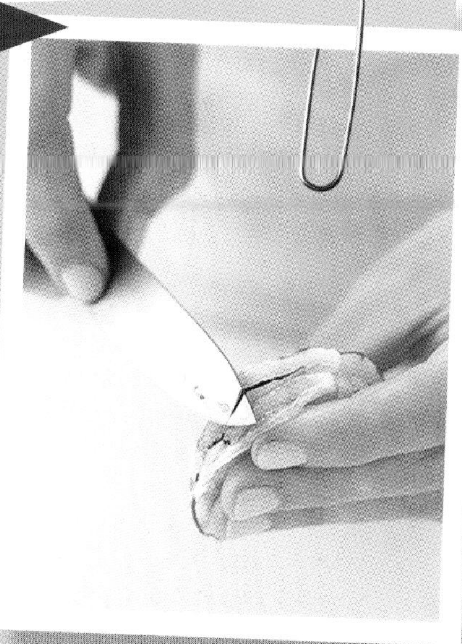

Tomato-Herb Pasta

You can also add cooked shrimp or chicken to this dish.

make ahead

MAKES 6 servings • **HANDS-ON TIME:** 30 min. • **TOTAL TIME:** 1 hr.

- **½ cup rice vinegar**
- **1 Tbsp. sugar**
- **½ medium-size red onion, thinly sliced**
- **½ (12-oz.) package whole grain spaghetti (we tested with Mueller's Whole Grain Spaghetti)**
- **2 medium tomatoes, seeded and chopped**
- **1 large cucumber, peeled and thinly sliced into half moons**
- **4 green onions, thinly sliced**
- **⅓ cup firmly packed fresh mint leaves, chopped**
- **⅓ cup firmly packed fresh cilantro leaves, chopped**
- **¼ cup fresh lime juice**
- **2 Tbsp. canola oil**
- **1 tsp. sugar**
- **1 tsp. salt**
- **½ tsp. dried crushed red pepper**
- **¼ cup chopped peanuts**

Garnish: fresh parsley

1. Whisk together vinegar and 1 Tbsp. sugar in a bowl. Add onion, and let stand 30 minutes; drain, reserving 2 Tbsp. vinegar mixture.

2. Prepare pasta according to package directions.

3. Place chopped tomatoes and next 9 ingredients in a serving bowl. Add hot cooked pasta, onion, and reserved vinegar mixture, gently tossing to combine. Sprinkle with peanuts. Serve immediately, or cover and chill up to 24 hours. Garnish, if desired.

Tuscan Pasta with Tomato-Basil Cream

MAKES 4 to 6 servings • **HANDS-ON TIME:** 10 min. • **TOTAL TIME:** 15 min.

- 1 (20-oz.) package refrigerated four-cheese ravioli* (we tested with Buitoni)
- 1 (16-oz.) jar sun-dried tomato Alfredo sauce (we tested with Classico)
- 2 Tbsp. white wine
- 2 medium-size fresh tomatoes, chopped**
- ½ cup chopped fresh basil
- ⅓ cup grated Parmesan cheese

Garnish: fresh basil strips

1. Prepare pasta according to package directions.
2. Meanwhile, pour Alfredo sauce into a medium saucepan. Pour wine into sauce jar; cover tightly, and shake well. Stir wine mixture into saucepan. Stir in chopped tomatoes and ½ cup chopped basil, and cook over medium-low heat 5 minutes or until thoroughly heated. Toss with pasta, and top evenly with ⅓ cup grated Parmesan cheese. Garnish, if desired.
*1 (13-oz.) package three-cheese tortellini may be substituted.
**1 (14.5-oz.) can petite diced tomatoes, fully drained, may be substituted.

Green Bean, Grape, and Pasta Toss

If you're a broccoli salad fan, you'll love the combination of these colorful ingredients. Cook the pasta al dente, so it's firm enough to hold its own when tossed with the tangy-sweet salad dressing.

MAKES 8 servings • **HANDS-ON TIME:** 37 min. • **TOTAL TIME:** 3 hr., 44 min.

make ahead

- 1 cup chopped pecans
- 8 bacon slices
- 1 lb. thin fresh green beans, trimmed and cut in half
- 1 (8-oz.) package penne pasta
- 1 cup mayonnaise
- ⅓ cup sugar
- ⅓ cup red wine vinegar
- 1 tsp. salt
- 2 cups seedless red grapes, cut in half
- ⅓ cup diced red onion
- Salt to taste

1. Preheat oven to 350°. Arrange pecans in a single layer on a baking sheet, and bake at 350° for 5 to 7 minutes or until lightly toasted and fragrant.
2. Cook bacon in a large skillet over medium-high heat 5 to 7 minutes or until crisp; remove bacon, and drain on paper towels. Crumble bacon.
3. Cook beans in boiling salted water to cover 5 minutes or until crisp-tender; drain. Plunge beans into ice water to stop the cooking process.
4. Meanwhile, prepare pasta according to package directions.
5. Whisk together mayonnaise and next 3 ingredients in a large bowl; add pecans, green beans, pasta, grapes, and onion, stirring to coat. Season with salt to taste. Cover and chill 3 hours; stir in bacon just before serving.

Pasta with White Beans and Arugula

MAKES 8 servings • **HANDS-ON TIME:** 15 min. • **TOTAL TIME:** 30 min.

30-minute special

- 1 (16-oz.) package farfalle (bow-tie) pasta
- 1 (19-oz.) can cannellini beans, drained and rinsed
- 1 (8.5-oz.) jar sun-dried tomatoes with herbs in oil, drained and chopped
- 1 (5-oz.) package fresh arugula, thoroughly washed
- 1 (4-oz.) package crumbled feta cheese
- ¼ cup chopped fresh basil
- 2 Tbsp. fresh lemon juice
- 2 Tbsp. olive oil
- ½ tsp. salt

1. Cook pasta according to package directions. Stir together beans and next 7 ingredients in a large bowl. Stir in hot cooked pasta until blended.

Pasta with Chickpeas, Tuna, and Arugula: Substitute 1 (16-oz.) can chickpeas, drained and rinsed, for cannellini beans. Stir in 3 (5-oz.) cans solid white tuna in water, drained.

Pasta with White Beans and Arugula

Vegetable-Pasta Oven Omelet

MAKES 8 servings • **HANDS-ON TIME:** 10 min. • **TOTAL TIME:** 45 min.

- 3 dried tomatoes in oil
- 1 small onion, chopped
- ½ red bell pepper, diced
- 3 garlic cloves, minced
- 2 Tbsp. olive oil
- 1 small zucchini, diced
- 1 (3-oz.) package cream cheese, softened
- 7 oz. vermicelli, cooked
- 6 large eggs
- ¾ cup (3 oz.) shredded Parmesan cheese, divided
- ¾ cup milk
- 1 tsp. dried Italian seasoning
- ½ tsp. salt
- ¼ tsp. pepper

1. Preheat oven to 375°. Drain tomatoes well, pressing between layers of paper towels; chop.
2. Sauté onion, bell pepper, and garlic in hot oil in a nonstick 12-inch ovenproof skillet 5 minutes or until tender; add tomato and zucchini, and sauté 3 minutes. Stir in cream cheese until melted. Add pasta; toss to coat.
3. Whisk together eggs, ½ cup Parmesan cheese, milk, and next 3 ingredients. Pour over pasta mixture in skillet.
4. Bake at 375° for 25 to 30 minutes or until set. Sprinkle with remaining ¼ cup Parmesan cheese. Let stand 10 minutes before serving.

Shrimp-and-Vegetable Oven Omelet: Toss 2 cups chopped cooked shrimp with pasta mixture. Continue as directed above.

Add a tossed garden salad and Italian bread to make a well-rounded supper.

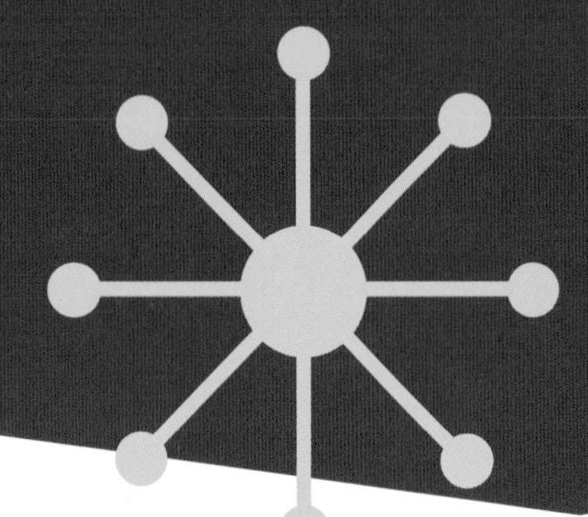

stir-fries and skillet SUPPERS

Beef-and-Vegetable Stir-Fry

MAKES 4 servings • **HANDS-ON TIME:** 35 min. • **TOTAL TIME:** 35 min.

- 1 lb. fresh asparagus
- 12 oz. top round steak, cut into thin strips
- 3 Tbsp. all-purpose flour
- ¼ cup soy sauce
- 2 garlic cloves, minced
- 1 Tbsp. dark sesame oil, divided
- 1 Tbsp. hoisin sauce
- ¼ tsp. dried crushed red pepper
- 4 small carrots, cut diagonally into ¼-inch-thick slices
- 1 small red bell pepper, cut into thin strips
- ½ cup sliced fresh mushrooms
- 5 green onions, cut into 1-inch pieces
- 2 cups hot cooked rice

1. Snap off tough ends of asparagus; cut spears into 1-inch pieces, and set aside.
2. Dredge steak in flour; set aside.
3. Stir together soy sauce, ¼ cup water, garlic, 1 tsp. sesame oil, hoisin sauce, and crushed red pepper.
4. Heat remaining 2 tsp. oil in a large skillet or wok over medium-high heat 2 minutes. Add beef and carrot, and stir-fry 4 minutes. Add soy sauce mixture, and stir-fry 1 minute. Add asparagus, bell pepper, mushrooms, and green onions, and stir-fry 3 minutes. Serve over rice.

Vegetable Stir-Fry: Omit round steak and flour, and stir-fry vegetables as directed above.

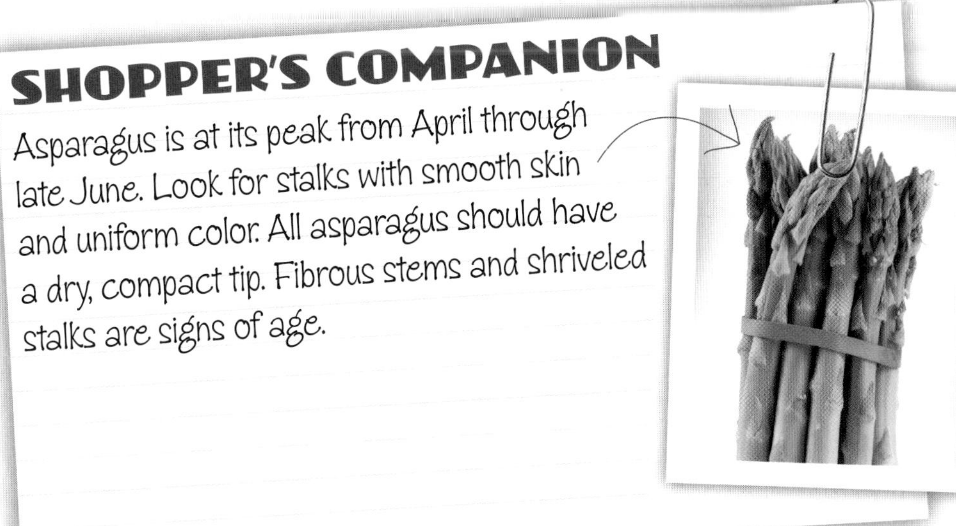

Thai Lemon Beef

MAKES 4 servings • **HANDS-ON TIME:** 20 min. • **TOTAL TIME:** 50 min.

- 1 (1-inch-thick) top round steak
- ⅓ cup soy sauce
- ¼ cup lemon juice
- 2 to 3 tsp. dried crushed red pepper
- 4 garlic cloves, minced
- 1 Tbsp. vegetable oil
- 4 green onions, cut into 2-inch pieces
- 2 carrots, thinly sliced
- 2 tsp. cornstarch
- Hot cooked ramen noodles
- Garnishes: lemon rind strips, fresh basil sprigs

1. Cut steak across the grain into ⅛-inch-thick strips, and place in a medium bowl.
2. Combine soy sauce, next 3 ingredients, and ¼ cup water. Reserve half of mixture. Pour remaining half of mixture over steak. Cover and chill 30 minutes.
3. Drain steak, discarding marinade.
4. Stir-fry half of steak in ½ Tbsp. hot oil in a large nonstick skillet or wok over medium-high heat 1 minute or until outside of beef is no longer pink. Remove from skillet, and repeat procedure with remaining oil and steak. Remove from skillet.
5. Add green onions and carrot to skillet, and stir-fry 3 minutes or until crisp-tender.
6. Whisk cornstarch into reserved soy sauce mixture; stir into vegetables, and stir-fry until thickened. Add steak, and stir-fry until thoroughly heated. Serve over noodles. Garnish, if desired.

How To Slice Beef Into Strips

When purchasing beef, look for a cherry red color, or—if it's vacuum-packed—a dark, purplish red color. The visible fat should be very white. The steak will be easier to slice if you partially freeze it first. Slice it diagonally across the grain into thin slices.

100 CALORIES
100 CALORIES
300 CALORIES
100 CALORIES
ALMONDS

Santa Fe Skillet Casserole

MAKES 6 servings • **HANDS-ON TIME:** 10 min. • **TOTAL TIME:** 15 min.

- 1 (12-oz.) package burger-style recipe crumbles
- 1 cup chopped onion (about 1)
- 1 cup chopped green bell pepper (about 1)
- 1½ cups uncooked instant rice (we tested with Uncle Ben's 5-Minute Rice)
- 1½ cups vegetable broth
- ¼ tsp. salt
- ¼ tsp. black pepper
- 1 (14.5-oz.) can Mexican-style stewed tomatoes, undrained
- ¾ cup (3 oz.) shredded 2% reduced-fat sharp Cheddar cheese

1. Combine first 3 ingredients in a large nonstick skillet; cook over medium-high heat until crumbles are browned and vegetables are tender.

2. Add rice and next 4 ingredients. Cover, reduce heat, and simmer 5 minutes or until rice is tender and liquid is absorbed. Sprinkle with cheese; serve immediately.

Substituting Mexican-seasoned burger-style crumbles for plain crumbles adds an extra kick to this one-dish meal.

Easy Skillet Tacos

Tacos are an easy go-to on a busy weeknight because all you have to do is prepare the beef and chop the toppings, and everyone can make their own. These tacos get their flavor from cumin and chili powder without the additional sodium often found in packaged seasoning mixes.

MAKES 4 to 6 servings • **HANDS-ON TIME:** 28 min. • **TOTAL TIME:** 40 min.

- **1 lb. ground beef**
- **1 small onion, chopped**
- **1 tsp. olive oil**
- **1 Tbsp. chili powder**
- **1½ tsp. ground cumin**
- **1 tsp. salt**
- **1 (15-oz.) can pinto beans, drained and rinsed**
- **1 (8-oz.) can tomato sauce**
- **½ cup salsa**
- **1½ cups (6 oz.) shredded Cheddar cheese**
- **1 Tbsp. chopped fresh cilantro**
- **Taco shells or flour tortillas, warmed**
- **Toppings: shredded lettuce, diced tomatoes, salsa, sour cream**

1. Cook ground beef in a large skillet over medium-high heat, stirring until beef crumbles and is no longer pink. Drain well. Remove beef; wipe skillet with a paper towel.
2. Sauté onion in hot oil in same skillet over medium-high heat. Add chili powder, cumin, salt, and beef. Cook 5 to 7 minutes, stirring occasionally. Stir in beans, tomato sauce, ¾ cup water, and salsa. Mash pinto beans in skillet with a fork, leaving some beans whole. Bring to a boil; reduce heat, and simmer, uncovered, 8 to 10 minutes or until liquid is reduced.
3. Top evenly with cheese and cilantro. Cover, turn off heat, and let stand 5 minutes or until cheese melts. Serve with taco shells or tortillas and desired toppings.

SHOPPER'S COMPANION

Also called coriander or Chinese parsley, cilantro has a pungent flavor. The leaves are often mistaken for flat-leaf parsley, so read the tag to verify that you're buying the correct herb.

Hot Sesame Pork on Mixed Greens

MAKES 8 servings • **HANDS-ON TIME:** 35 min. • **TOTAL TIME:** 35 min.

- **½ (16-oz.) package wonton wrappers**
- **2 lb. boneless pork loin, trimmed**
- **¾ cup sesame seeds, divided**
- **1 cup vegetable oil, divided**
- **½ cup all-purpose flour**
- **1 tsp. salt**
- **½ tsp. pepper**
- **¼ cup dark sesame oil, divided**
- **½ cup firmly packed brown sugar**
- **⅓ cup soy sauce**
- **¼ cup rice vinegar**
- **10 to 12 small green onions, sliced**
- **2 (5-oz.) packages mixed salad greens**
- **1 bok choy, shredded**

1. Cut wonton wrappers into ½-inch strips, and cut pork into 3- x 1-inch strips; set aside.
2. Toast ½ cup sesame seeds in a large heavy skillet over medium-high heat, stirring constantly, 2 to 3 minutes; remove from skillet.
3. Pour ½ cup vegetable oil into skillet; heat to 375°. Fry wonton strips in batches until golden. Drain on paper towels; set aside. Drain skillet.
4. Combine remaining ¼ cup sesame seeds, flour, salt, and pepper in a zip-top plastic freezer bag; add pork. Seal and shake to coat.
5. Pour 2 Tbsp. sesame oil into skillet; place over medium heat. Fry half of pork in hot oil, stirring often, 6 to 8 minutes or until golden. Remove and keep warm. Repeat procedure with remaining 2 Tbsp. sesame oil and pork.
6. Process toasted sesame seeds, remaining ½ cup vegetable oil, ½ cup brown sugar, soy sauce, and vinegar in a blender 1 to 2 minutes or until smooth.
7. Combine pork and green onions; drizzle with soy sauce mixture, tossing gently.
8. Combine mixed greens and bok choy; top with pork mixture and fried wonton strips. Serve immediately.

How To Slice Green Onions

Diagonally sliced green onions make an eye-catching garnish or addition to a recipe. Slice green onions diagonally by holding the knife at a 45-degree angle to the green onions and slicing to the desired thickness.

Pork Fried Rice

MAKES 6 servings • **HANDS-ON TIME:** 30 min. • **TOTAL TIME:** 30 min.

- 1 lb. boneless pork chops, cut into strips
- ½ tsp. pepper
- 1 Tbsp. sesame oil, divided
- ¾ cup diced carrots
- ½ cup chopped onion
- 3 green onions, chopped
- 1 Tbsp. butter
- 2 large eggs, lightly beaten
- 2 cups cooked long-grain white or jasmine rice, chilled
- ½ cup frozen English peas, thawed (optional)
- ¼ cup soy sauce
- Garnishes: green onion, carrot

1. Season pork with pepper. Cook pork in 1½ tsp. hot sesame oil in a large skillet over medium heat 7 to 8 minutes or until done. Remove pork from skillet.

2. Heat remaining 1½ tsp. sesame oil in skillet; sauté carrot and onion in hot oil 2 to 3 minutes or until tender. Stir in green onions, and sauté 1 minute. Remove mixture from skillet. Wipe skillet clean.

3. Melt butter in skillet. Add eggs to skillet, and cook, without stirring, 1 minute or until eggs begin to set on bottom. Gently draw cooked edges away from sides of pan to form large pieces. Cook, stirring occasionally, 30 seconds to 1 minute or until thickened and moist. (Do not overstir.) Add pork, carrot mixture, rice, and, if desired, peas to skillet; cook over medium heat, stirring often, 2 to 3 minutes or until thoroughly heated. Stir in soy sauce. Serve immediately. Garnish, if desired.

SHORTCUT SECRET

You can make the rice ahead of time. In fact, chilling the rice will help keep it from clumping while stir-frying. Use leftover rice, or prepare 1 (8-oz.) pouch ready-to-serve jasmine rice according to package directions, and chill.

Skillet Sausage 'n' Rice

MAKES 4 to 6 servings • **HANDS-ON TIME:** 10 min. • **TOTAL TIME:** 30 min.

- 1 (16-oz.) package smoked sausage
- 1 medium-size green bell pepper, chopped
- 1 small onion, chopped
- 1 garlic clove, minced
- 1 cup chicken broth
- 2 (3.5-oz.) bags quick-cooking brown rice
- ½ tsp. salt
- ¼ tsp. black pepper
- Garnish: chopped fresh parsley

1. Cut sausage into ½-inch slices. Sauté in a large nonstick skillet over medium-high heat 8 to 10 minutes or until lightly browned. Remove sausage slices, and drain on paper towels, reserving 1 Tbsp. drippings in skillet.

2. Add bell pepper, onion, and garlic to skillet, and sauté over medium-high heat 4 minutes or until tender. Add chicken broth, stirring to loosen particles from bottom of skillet, and bring to a boil. Remove rice from cooking bags; add rice, sausage, salt, and black pepper to skillet. Reduce heat to medium-low, cover, and cook 5 minutes or until rice is tender. Garnish, if desired.

SHOPPER'S COMPANION

Shop for green bell peppers that have bright colors and taut skin, and are free of any dark spots. Make sure that the pepper is firm and sturdy, avoiding peppers that show signs of decay. Peppers can be found all year long, but are most abundant during the summer months. To make cooking even faster, purchase prechopped bell peppers from the produce section of your grocery store.

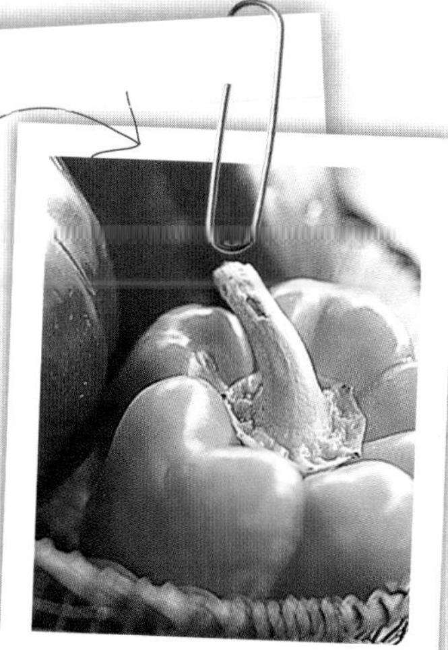

Easy Skillet Cordon Bleu

MAKES 4 to 6 servings • **HANDS-ON TIME:** 10 min. • **TOTAL TIME:** 20 min.

- ½ cup Italian-seasoned breadcrumbs
- 1 tsp. pepper
- ½ tsp. salt
- 8 chicken tenders (about 1 lb.)
- 1 Tbsp. butter
- 1 Tbsp. olive oil
- 8 Canadian bacon slices, cut into thin strips
- 4 Swiss cheese slices, halved

1. Combine breadcrumbs, pepper, and salt in a large zip-top plastic freezer bag. Rinse chicken tenders, and add to freezer bag. Seal bag, and shake to coat.
2. Melt butter with oil in an ovenproof skillet over medium heat. Cook chicken 3½ to 4 minutes on each side or until done. Arrange Canadian bacon strips over chicken in skillet, and top each with 1 cheese slice. Broil 5½ inches from heat 2 minutes or until cheese is melted.

Pasta with Broccoli and Sausage

MAKES 4 servings • **HANDS-ON TIME:** 22 min. • **TOTAL TIME:** 37 min.

- 1 lb. fresh broccoli, cut into florets
- 1 (9-oz.) package refrigerated fettuccine
- 2 Tbsp. butter
- 1 cup sliced fresh mushrooms
- 1 garlic clove, minced
- 1 lb. reduced-fat smoked sausage, sliced
- 3 large eggs
- ¾ cup whipping cream
- ¾ tsp. pepper
- 1 cup grated Parmesan cheese

1. Cook broccoli and fettuccine in boiling water to cover in a Dutch oven 4 minutes or until broccoli is crisp-tender; drain. Rinse with cold water; drain. Place in a large bowl.
2. Melt butter in a large heavy skillet; add mushrooms and garlic, and sauté 3 minutes or until tender. Add to fettuccine mixture.
3. Brown sausage in skillet over medium-high heat, stirring occasionally, 5 minutes; drain and add to fettuccine mixture. Wipe skillet clean with a paper towel.
4. Stir together eggs, whipping cream, and pepper in skillet until blended. Add fettuccine mixture; toss well. Cook over low heat, stirring constantly, 3 to 5 minutes or until thickened. Sprinkle with Parmesan cheese, and toss. Serve immediately.

Pasta with Broccoli and Sausage

Sausage-and-Chicken Cassoulet

A cassoulet is a French dish of beans, sausages, and meat that's covered and slowly cooked. Our Test Kitchens' version is covered with a cornbread crust. Check your cookware information to make sure your skillet's handle is ovenproof up to 400° or higher. If not, just prep in a traditional skillet and then bake in a casserole dish that holds 2¼ to 3 quarts. (You can measure your dish capacity using water if the dish is not labeled.) We used a Le Creuset 2¼-qt. (8½-inch-diameter x 3-inch-deep) Saucier Pan at one testing and a hand-me-down 3-qt. (10-inch-diameter x 3-inch-deep) cast-iron skillet at another testing. Both skillets worked fine.

MAKES 6 servings • **HANDS-ON TIME:** 25 min. • **TOTAL TIME:** 1 hr., 30 min.

- **1 (16-oz.) package smoked sausage, sliced**
- **1 lb. skinned, boned chicken breasts, chopped**
- **1 (15.8-oz.) can great Northern beans, drained and rinsed**
- **1 (14.5-oz.) can diced tomatoes with onion and garlic, drained**
- **1 (14-oz.) can chicken broth**
- **1½ tsp. dried thyme**
- **1 (6-oz.) package buttermilk cornbread mix (we tested with Martha White)**
- **⅔ cup water or milk**

1. Preheat oven to 400°. Cook sausage in a 2¼- to 3-qt. ovenproof skillet over medium heat 8 minutes or until browned. Remove sausage from skillet, and drain on paper towels, reserving drippings in skillet. Set sausage aside.
2. Cook chicken in hot drippings in skillet over medium-high heat 5 minutes or until brown.
3. Return sausage to skillet with chicken. Stir in beans and next 3 ingredients. Bring to a boil.
4. Stir together cornbread mix and ⅔ cup water or milk. Pour evenly over hot sausage mixture in skillet.
5. Bake at 400° for 30 to 35 minutes or until golden. Let stand 10 minutes before serving.

Chicken Scaloppine with Spinach and Linguine

MAKES 6 servings • **HANDS-ON TIME:** 25 min. • **TOTAL TIME:** 45 min.

- 1 lb. fresh asparagus
- 1 (16-oz.) package linguine
- 1 (9-oz.) package fresh spinach, thoroughly washed
- ¾ cup all-purpose flour
- 2 tsp. salt, divided
- 1½ tsp. pepper, divided
- 6 chicken cutlets (about 1½ lb.)
- 2 Tbsp. butter
- 2 Tbsp. olive oil
- 2 Tbsp. all-purpose flour
- 2½ cups chicken broth
- 1 Tbsp. lemon zest
- 3 Tbsp. fresh lemon juice
- ¼ cup capers, drained and rinsed
- 2 plum tomatoes, seeded and chopped
- Grated Parmesan cheese

1. Snap off and discard tough ends of asparagus; cut asparagus in half crosswise.

2. Prepare linguine according to package directions, adding asparagus during last 2 minutes of cooking. Drain; return to pan. Stir in spinach; cover and keep warm over low heat.

3. Combine ¾ cup flour, 1½ tsp. salt, and 1 tsp. pepper in a large zip-top plastic bag. Add chicken cutlets; seal bag, and shake to lightly coat.

4. Melt 1 Tbsp. butter with 1 Tbsp. olive oil in a large nonstick skillet over medium-high heat. Cook 3 cutlets in skillet 2 to 3 minutes; turn and cook 2 to 3 minutes or until lightly browned and done. Remove from skillet. Repeat procedure with remaining 1 Tbsp. butter, 1 Tbsp. oil, and 3 cutlets. (Chicken may be kept warm in a 250° oven on a wire rack.)

5. Whisk 2 Tbsp. flour into skillet, and cook 30 seconds. Whisk in chicken broth, next 3 ingredients, and remaining ½ tsp. salt and ½ tsp. pepper. Cook over medium-high heat 6 to 8 minutes or until slightly thickened, whisking to loosen particles from bottom of skillet. Pour over warm pasta mixture; toss to combine. Transfer to a serving dish, and sprinkle with tomatoes. Serve immediately with chicken and Parmesan cheese.

Use Parmigiano-Reggiano cheese. Allow your guests to grate the cheese tableside right onto their plates.

Mexican Bow-Tie Pasta with Chicken

You can use almost any shape of pasta in this recipe. Penne, rigatoni, and elbow macaroni work particularly well.

30-minute special

MAKES 6 servings • **HANDS-ON TIME:** 25 min. • **TOTAL TIME:** 25 min.

- 1 lb. uncooked farfalle (bow-tie) pasta
- 1½ lb. skinned and boned chicken thighs or breasts
- 2 Tbsp. butter
- 2 garlic cloves, crushed
- ¼ cup all-purpose flour
- 1 cup chicken broth
- ½ cup milk
- 1 cup salsa
- 1 (8-oz.) package cream cheese, cut into ½-inch cubes

1. Cook pasta according to package directions. Drain and set aside.
2. Meanwhile, cut chicken into bite-size pieces. Melt butter in a large skillet over medium heat. Add chicken; cook, stirring constantly, 4 to 5 minutes. Add garlic and continue to cook until chicken is just cooked through. Stir in flour; slowly pour in broth and milk, stirring constantly. Add salsa and cream cheese; stir until sauce is hot and bubbling and cream cheese is melted and smooth.
3. Add drained pasta to skillet; stir until pasta is coated with sauce and everything is well combined. Serve immediately.

Creole Fried Rice

MAKES 6 servings • **HANDS-ON TIME:** 56 min. • **TOTAL TIME:** 1 hr., 26 min.

- 1 cup uncooked long-grain rice
- 2 cups chicken broth
- 1 lb. skinned and boned chicken thighs
- 1½ tsp. Creole seasoning, divided
- 2 Tbsp. vegetable oil
- ½ lb. andouille or smoked sausage, sliced
- ½ small onion, chopped
- ½ small green bell pepper, chopped
- 2 garlic cloves, chopped
- 1 cup frozen sliced okra, thawed
- 3 plum tomatoes, chopped
- 2 green onions, sliced (green part only)

1. Cook rice according to package directions, substituting 2 cups chicken broth for water. Spread cooked rice in a thin layer on a baking sheet. Let cool 30 minutes or until completely cool.
2. Cut chicken thighs into 1-inch pieces, and toss with 1 tsp. Creole seasoning.
3. Cook chicken in hot oil in a large skillet over medium heat 3 minutes; add sausage, and cook 3 to 4 minutes or until lightly browned. Add onion, bell pepper, and garlic, and cook 5 minutes or until onion is tender. Stir in okra and remaining ½ tsp. Creole seasoning. Increase heat to high; add rice, and cook, stirring constantly, 4 minutes or until thoroughly heated. Stir in tomatoes. Sprinkle with sliced green onions, and serve immediately.

Creole Fried Rice

Szechuan Chicken and Vegetables

Szechuan Chicken and Vegetables

Create your own combo of fresh stir-fry vegetables from the salad bar at the grocery store.

30-minute special

MAKES 4 servings • **HANDS-ON TIME:** 10 min. • **TOTAL TIME:** 10 min.

- **2 tsp. dark or light sesame oil**
- **1 lb. chicken breast tenders**
- **¼ tsp. dried crushed red pepper**
- **1 (10-oz.) package fresh stir-fry vegetables (about 2½ cups)**
- **¼ cup low-sodium teriyaki sauce**

1. Heat oil in a large nonstick skillet over medium-high heat. Add chicken, and sprinkle with crushed red pepper; stir-fry 3 minutes.
2. Add vegetables and teriyaki sauce; stir-fry 5 minutes or until vegetables are crisp-tender and chicken is thoroughly cooked.

Chicken and Sausage Jambalaya

30-minute special

MAKES 6 servings • **HANDS-ON TIME:** 30 min. • **TOTAL TIME:** 30 min.

- **1 lb. skinned and boned chicken breasts, cut into 1-inch pieces**
- **2 tsp. Cajun seasoning, divided**
- **2 tsp. canola oil**
- **1 lb. smoked sausage, sliced**
- **1 (10-oz.) package frozen seasoning blend, thawed and drained**
- **2 tsp. jarred minced garlic**
- **1 (14½-oz.) can diced tomatoes with zesty mild green chiles, undrained**
- **1 extra-large bag boil-in-bag white rice, removed from bag**
- **1½ cups chicken broth**
- **Garnish: minced flat-leaf parsley**

1. Combine chicken and 1 tsp. Cajun seasoning in a bowl.
2. Heat oil in a Dutch oven over medium-high heat. Add sausage and chicken; sauté 6 minutes or until browned on all sides. Remove from pan; drain.
3. Add seasoning blend and garlic to pan; sauté 2 minutes or until thoroughly heated. Add sausage, chicken, remaining 1 tsp. Cajun seasoning, tomatoes, rice, and broth to pan. Bring to a boil; cover and boil 11 minutes or until liquid is absorbed, stirring halfway through cooking time. Garnish, if desired.

Skillet-Grilled Burritos

MAKES 8 servings • **HANDS-ON TIME:** 28 min. • **TOTAL TIME:** 1 hr., 8 min., including sauce

2 cups chopped cooked chicken breast
1 (15-oz.) can black beans, drained and rinsed
1 (11-oz.) can yellow corn with red and green bell peppers, drained
1 cup (4 oz.) shredded 2% reduced-fat Cheddar cheese
Creamy Cilantro-Jalapeño Sauce
8 (8-inch) soft taco-size whole wheat flour tortillas, warmed
Vegetable cooking spray
Salsa

1. Toss together first 4 ingredients and ½ cup Creamy Cilantro-Jalapeño Sauce. Spread ¾ cup chicken mixture just below center of each tortilla. Fold opposite sides of tortillas over filling, and roll up. Coat burritos with cooking spray.
2. Coat a hot griddle or nonstick skillet with cooking spray. Cook burritos, in batches, on hot griddle over medium heat, pressing gently with a spatula, 3 to 4 minutes on each side or until golden brown and cheese is melted. Serve with salsa and remaining Creamy Cilantro-Jalapeño Sauce.

Creamy Cilantro-Jalapeño Sauce

MAKES 1¼ cups • **HANDS-ON TIME:** 10 min. • **TOTAL TIME:** 40 min.

1 cup light sour cream
½ cup loosely packed fresh cilantro leaves, chopped
2 Tbsp. diced pickled jalapeño peppers
2 tsp. chopped yellow onion
2 tsp. Dijon mustard
1 tsp. lime zest

1. Stir together all ingredients in a small bowl. Cover and chill 30 minutes. Store in an airtight container up to 2 days.

How To Fill and Fold a Burrito

Simply spread the mixture just below the center of each tortilla, and fold the left and right sides of the tortillas while rolling up. Then place the burritos, seam side down, onto a hot griddle or skillet, and brown on each side for a crispy, melt-in-your-mouth main dish.

Garlic Turkey-Broccoli Stir-Fry

MAKES 4 servings • **HANDS-ON TIME:** 6 min. • **TOTAL TIME:** 14 min.

- 2 tsp. sesame oil, divided
- 1 (1-lb.) turkey tenderloin, cut into thin strips
- 1 cup chicken broth
- 4 garlic cloves, minced
- 1½ Tbsp. cornstarch
- ¼ tsp. dried crushed red pepper
- ¼ tsp. salt
- 1 red bell pepper, cut into thin strips
- 2 cups fresh broccoli florets
- 1 (8-oz.) can sliced water chestnuts, drained
- 2 Tbsp. soy sauce
- 2 cups hot cooked rice

1. Place a large nonstick skillet over medium-high heat until hot. Add 1 tsp. sesame oil to pan, and tilt to coat evenly. Add turkey, and stir-fry 5 minutes or until turkey is no longer pink in center. Remove turkey, and set aside.
2. Combine broth and next 4 ingredients in a small bowl; stir until cornstarch dissolves. Set aside.
3. Add remaining 1 tsp. oil to pan. Add pepper strips and broccoli; stir-fry 1 minute.
4. Add water chestnuts, and stir-fry 30 seconds. Increase heat to high. Stir broth mixture, and add to pan with soy sauce, turkey, and any accumulated juices. Bring to a boil; cook 1 to 2 minutes or until slightly thickened. Serve over rice.

Spicy Catfish with Vegetables and Basil Cream

MAKES 4 servings • **HANDS-ON TIME:** 25 min. • **TOTAL TIME:** 25 min.

- **3 Tbsp. butter, divided**
- **1 (16-oz.) package frozen whole kernel corn, thawed**
- **1 medium onion, chopped**
- **1 medium-size green bell pepper, chopped**
- **1 medium-size red bell pepper, chopped**
- **¾ tsp. salt**
- **¾ tsp. black pepper**
- **4 (6- to 8-oz.) catfish fillets**
- **½ cup all-purpose flour, plus 2 Tbsp., divided**
- **¼ cup yellow cornmeal**
- **1 Tbsp. Creole seasoning**
- **⅓ cup buttermilk**
- **1 Tbsp. vegetable oil**
- **½ cup whipping cream**
- **2 Tbsp. chopped fresh basil**

1. Melt 2 Tbsp. butter in a large skillet over medium-high heat. Add corn, onion, and bell peppers; sauté 6 to 8 minutes or until tender. Stir in salt and black pepper; spoon onto a serving dish, and keep warm.
2. Dredge fillets in 2 Tbsp. flour. Combine ½ cup flour, cornmeal, and Creole seasoning in a large shallow dish. Dip fillets in buttermilk, and dredge in flour mixture.
3. Melt remaining 1 Tbsp. butter with oil in skillet over medium-high heat. Cook fillets, in batches, 2 to 3 minutes on each side or until golden. Remove fillets from skillet and arrange over vegetables.
4. Add cream to skillet, stirring to loosen particles from bottom of skillet. Add chopped basil, and cook, stirring often, 1 to 2 minutes or until thickened. Serve sauce with fillets and vegetables.

SHORTCUT SECRET

The key when breading fish is to use one hand for the wet ingredients and one hand for the dry. Dip a fillet in the milk (or wet mixture). Then, with your dry hand, dredge the fillet in the flour. This technique prevents your hands from becoming covered in breading mixture.

Curried Rice with Shrimp

This Indian-style meal goes together very quickly and feels like a nice treat. Add more curry powder if you like it spicy.

30-minute special

MAKES 4 servings • **HANDS-ON TIME:** 25 min. • **TOTAL TIME:** 25 min.

- 2 Tbsp. olive oil
- 1 large onion, finely chopped
- 2 carrots, thinly sliced
- 2 russet potatoes, peeled and cut into 1-inch cubes
- 2½ cups chicken broth, divided
- 2 garlic cloves, minced
- 2 tsp. curry powder
- 1 cup uncooked long-grain white rice
- ½ tsp. black pepper
- 1 lb. medium-size shrimp, peeled and deveined
- ¼ cup chopped fresh basil or 2 tsp. dried

1. Heat oil in a large skillet over medium heat until hot. Add onion, carrot, and potato; cook, stirring occasionally, until vegetables start to soften, 6 to 8 minutes. If vegetables begin to stick, add a little slosh of chicken broth to skillet.
2. Add garlic and curry powder; cook, stirring until fragrant, about 2 minutes. Add rice, broth, and pepper. Bring to a boil. Reduce heat to medium-low, cover, and simmer 15 minutes.
3. Add shrimp; stir, cover, and cook, stirring occasionally, until shrimp are opaque and rice is tender, about 5 to 7 minutes. Sprinkle with basil, and serve immediately.

SHOPPER'S COMPANION

High-tech methods of freezing lock in fresh flavor, providing a quality selection of fish and shellfish year-round. Look for packages that are clean and tightly sealed, with no signs of freezer burn. Allow 24 hours to thaw a 1-lb. package of frozen fish or shellfish in the refrigerator. Speeding up the process by thawing at room temperature or under running water drains the moisture and breaks down the texture of the fish or shellfish.

Sunny Skillet Breakfast

Soaking the shredded potatoes in cold water keeps them from turning gray before cooking. It also rinses off some of the starch. Drain and pat them dry, so they won't stick to the cast-iron skillet.

MAKES 6 servings • **HANDS-ON TIME:** 15 min. • **TOTAL TIME:** 50 min.

- **3 (8-oz.) baking potatoes, peeled and shredded (about 3 cups firmly packed)***
- **1 Tbsp. butter**
- **2 Tbsp. vegetable oil**
- **1 small red bell pepper, diced**
- **1 medium onion, diced**
- **1 garlic clove, pressed**
- **¾ tsp. salt, divided**
- **6 large eggs**
- **¼ tsp. black pepper**

1. Preheat oven to 350°. Place shredded potatoes in a large bowl; add cold water to cover. Let stand 5 minutes; drain and pat dry.
2. Melt butter with oil in a 10-inch cast-iron skillet over medium heat. Add bell pepper and onion, and sauté 3 to 5 minutes or until tender. Add garlic; sauté 1 minute. Stir in shredded potatoes and ½ tsp. salt; cook, stirring often, 10 minutes or until potatoes are golden and tender.
3. Remove from heat. Make 6 indentations in potato mixture, using back of a spoon. Break 1 egg into each indentation. Sprinkle eggs with black pepper and remaining ¼ tsp. salt.
4. Bake at 350° for 12 to 14 minutes or until eggs are set. Serve immediately.
*3 cups firmly packed frozen shredded potatoes may be substituted, omitting Step 1.

Veggie Confetti Frittata: Prepare recipe as directed through Step 2, sautéing ½ (8-oz.) package sliced fresh mushrooms with bell pepper and onion. Remove from heat, and stir in ¼ cup sliced ripe black olives, drained, and ¼ cup thinly sliced sun-dried tomatoes in oil, drained. Whisk together eggs, black pepper, and remaining ¼ tsp. salt; whisk in ½ cup (2 oz.) shredded Swiss cheese. Pour egg mixture over potato mixture in skillet. Bake at 350° for 9 to 10 minutes or until set. Cut into wedges, and serve immediately.

Thai Fried Rice with Tofu

This quick dish gets a smoky flavor boost from packaged pregrilled tofu. Like most fried rice dishes, leftovers are even better the next day.

30-minute special

MAKES 4 servings • **HANDS-ON TIME:** 26 min. • **TOTAL TIME:** 26 min.

- 2 tsp. peanut oil
- 2 tsp. jarred minced ginger
- 1 tsp. jarred minced garlic
- ½ tsp. dried crushed red pepper
- 1 (9.2-oz.) package original grilled tofu, cut into ½-inch pieces (we tested with Marjon)
- ¼ cup sweetened flaked coconut, toasted
- 1 Tbsp. light brown sugar
- 1 large egg, lightly beaten
- 3 cups coarsely chopped bok choy (about 1 large head)
- 1½ cups frozen cut green beans, thawed
- ¼ cup chopped dry-roasted salted cashews
- 2 cups chilled cooked jasmine or basmati rice
- 2 Tbsp. soy sauce

1. Heat oil in a large nonstick skillet over medium-high heat. Add ginger and next 3 ingredients; sauté 3 minutes. Add coconut and brown sugar; cook 1 minute. Push tofu mixture to one side of pan. Add egg to empty side of pan; stir-fry 1 to 2 minutes or until soft-scrambled.
2. Add bok choy, green beans, and cashews, and cook 5 minutes or until vegetables are tender, stirring occasionally. Stir in rice and soy sauce, and cook 2 minutes or until thoroughly heated.

SHORTCUT SECRET

The rice for this recipe was prepared ahead and chilled overnight. It was cooked in the microwave according to package directions, omitting salt and fat. Use ⅔ cup uncooked rice and 1⅓ cups water to get a 2-cup yield of cooked rice. If you have any kind of leftover cooked rice from another meal, you may substitute it for the jasmine rice, if desired.

Peanut-Broccoli Stir-Fry

Peanut-Broccoli Stir-Fry

MAKES 6 servings • **HANDS-ON TIME:** 30 min. • **TOTAL TIME:** 1 hr., 15 min.

- **1 (16-oz.) package firm tofu**
- **2 cups uncooked brown rice**
- **½ tsp. salt**
- **1½ cups vegetable broth**
- **1 Tbsp. light brown sugar**
- **2 Tbsp. fresh lime juice**
- **2 Tbsp. sweet chili sauce**
- **2 Tbsp. creamy peanut butter**
- **1 Tbsp. lite soy sauce**
- **1 tsp. grated fresh ginger**
- **¾ tsp. cornstarch**
- **1 Tbsp. peanut or vegetable oil**
- **1 tsp. dark sesame oil**
- **2 cups fresh broccoli florets**
- **1 cup matchstick carrots**
- **2 Tbsp. chopped peanuts**

1. Place tofu between 2 flat plates. Weight the top with a heavy can. (Sides of tofu should be bulging slightly but not cracking.) Let stand 45 minutes; discard liquid. Cut tofu into ½-inch cubes.
2. Prepare rice according to package directions, adding ½ tsp. salt.
3. Meanwhile, combine vegetable broth and next 7 ingredients in a medium bowl, stirring well. Add tofu, and toss to coat. Let stand 10 minutes. Remove tofu from marinade, reserving marinade.
4. Heat oils in a nonstick skillet or wok over high heat 1 minute. Add tofu, and stir-fry 4 to 5 minutes or until browned. Remove tofu. Add broccoli and matchstick carrots; stir-fry 2 minutes. Add reserved marinade, and bring to a boil. Cook, stirring constantly, 2 minutes or until thickened; stir in cooked tofu. Serve over hot cooked rice. Sprinkle with chopped peanuts.

Skillet Veggie Tacos

MAKES 12 servings • **HANDS-ON TIME:** 15 min. • **TOTAL TIME:** 35 min.

- **2 red bell peppers, coarsely chopped**
- **1 medium onion, chopped**
- **1 cup sliced fresh mushrooms**
- **1 to 2 jalapeño peppers, seeded and chopped**
- **2 garlic cloves, minced**
- **2 tsp. olive oil**
- **1½ tsp. ground cumin**
- **1 tsp. dried oregano**
- **¾ cup sweet white wine**
- **1 (15-oz.) can pinto beans, drained and rinsed**
- **2 cups chopped fresh spinach**
- **12 (8-inch) fat-free flour tortillas, warmed**
- **½ cup crumbled reduced-fat feta cheese (optional)**

1. Sauté first 5 ingredients in hot oil in a skillet over medium-high heat 5 minutes or until vegetables are tender. Add cumin and oregano; sauté 2 minutes.
2. Stir in wine; reduce heat, and simmer 10 minutes or until liquid is reduced by half. Add beans, and cook until thoroughly heated. Add spinach; cook 2 minutes or until spinach wilts. Serve in warm tortillas with cheese, if desired.

Ricotta and Spinach Tortelloni with Summer Vegetables

Feel free to toss in other fresh vegetables such as squash, broccoli, green beans, or mushrooms. Cut vegetables ahead of time, wrap in damp paper towels, and place in a zip-top plastic bag. Chill up to 1 day.

30-minute special

MAKES 4 servings • **HANDS-ON TIME:** 15 min. • **TOTAL TIME:** 30 min.

- 1 (8-oz.) package ricotta and spinach tortelloni
- ¼ tsp. minced garlic
- 2 Tbsp. extra virgin olive oil
- 1 red bell pepper, cut into ½-inch strips
- 1 carrot, cut into ½-inch strips
- 1 zucchini, cut into ½-inch strips
- ½ medium onion, diced
- Salt and black pepper to taste
- 3 Tbsp. grated Parmesan cheese

1. Cook tortelloni according to package directions; drain and keep warm.
2. While pasta cooks, sauté garlic in hot oil in a large skillet over medium heat 3 minutes. Add red bell pepper and next 3 ingredients, and sauté 8 to 9 minutes. Stir in ¼ cup water and salt and black pepper to taste.
3. Toss together tortelloni, vegetable mixture, and cheese until blended. Serve immediately.

Easy Skillet Pimiento Mac 'n' Cheese

healthy & hearty

MAKES 6 servings • **HANDS-ON TIME:** 10 min. • **TOTAL TIME:** 20 min.

- ½ (16-oz.) package penne pasta
- 2 Tbsp. all-purpose flour
- 1½ cups 1% low-fat milk
- 1 cup (4 oz.) shredded sharp Cheddar cheese
- 1 (4-oz.) jar diced pimiento, drained
- ¾ tsp. salt
- ¼ tsp. pepper
- Pinch of paprika

1. Prepare pasta according to package directions.
2. Whisk together flour and ¼ cup milk. Add flour mixture to remaining milk, whisking until smooth.
3. Bring milk mixture to a boil in a large skillet over medium heat; reduce heat to medium-low, and simmer, whisking constantly, 3 to 5 minutes or until smooth. Stir in cheese and next 4 ingredients until smooth. Stir in pasta, and cook 1 minute or until thoroughly heated. Serve immediately.

Easy Skillet Green Chile Mac 'n' Cheese: Substitute 1 cup (4 oz.) shredded Monterey Jack cheese for Cheddar cheese and 1 (4-oz.) can chopped green chiles, undrained, for diced pimiento. Proceed with recipe as directed.

Easy Skillet Whole Grain Mac 'n' Cheese: Substitute ½ (13.5-oz.) package whole grain penne pasta for regular. Proceed with recipe as directed.

Easy Skillet Pimiento Mac 'n' Cheese

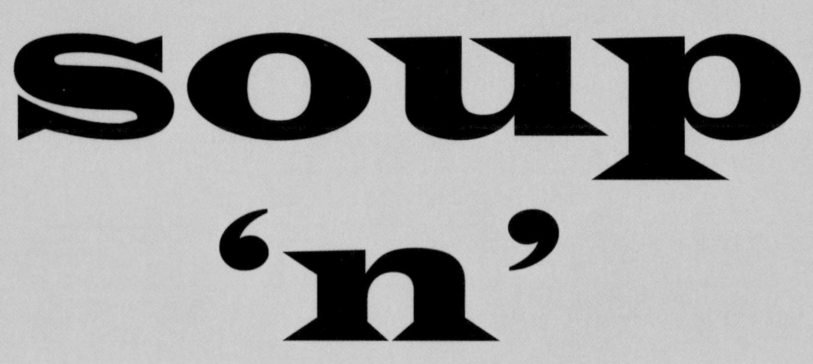

salad

SUPPERS

Southern Tortellini Minestrone

MAKES 8 to 10 servings • **HANDS-ON TIME:** 20 min. • **TOTAL TIME:** 1 hr., 2 min.

- 1 medium onion, chopped
- 1 Tbsp. olive oil
- 3 garlic cloves, chopped
- 2 (32-oz.) containers chicken broth
- ¾ cup dry white wine
- 2 (14.5-oz.) cans Italian-style diced tomatoes
- 1 (16-oz.) package frozen green beans
- 1 (16-oz.) package frozen chopped collard greens
- 3 Tbsp. chopped fresh parsley
- 1 Tbsp. chopped fresh rosemary
- ½ tsp. dried crushed red pepper
- 1 (16-oz.) package frozen cheese tortellini

Garnish: black pepper

1. Sauté onion in hot oil in a large Dutch oven over medium heat 8 minutes or until onion is tender. Add garlic, and cook 1 minute. Stir in chicken broth, white wine, and tomatoes; bring to a boil over medium-high heat. Add green beans, collard greens, and next 3 ingredients. Reduce heat to medium, and simmer, stirring occasionally, 15 minutes. Add pasta, and cook 10 to 12 minutes or until pasta is done. Garnish, if desired.

SHOPPER'S COMPANION

Keep in mind that frozen vegetables labeled Grade A by the USDA are the most tender and flavorful. Less expensive Grade B vegetables are more mature, but still a quality buy. Super-thrifty Grade C vegetables are best used in long-simmering soups or stews.

Beefy Minestrone Soup

MAKES 6 servings • **HANDS-ON TIME:** 3 min. • **TOTAL TIME:** 13 min.

- ⅔ cup uncooked ditalini (very short, tube-shaped macaroni)
- 2 (14-oz.) cans low-sodium fat-free beef broth
- 1 (14.5-oz.) can no-salt-added stewed tomatoes, undrained
- 1 large zucchini
- 1 (15.5-oz.) can cannellini beans or other white beans, drained and rinsed
- 2 tsp. dried Italian seasoning
- 8 oz. deli rare roast beef, sliced ¼ inch thick and diced

1. Combine first 3 ingredients in a large saucepan; cover and bring to a boil over high heat.
2. Cut zucchini in half lengthwise, and slice. Add zucchini, beans, and Italian seasoning to pasta; cover, reduce heat, and simmer 6 minutes. Add beef, and cook 4 minutes or until pasta is tender.

SHOPPER'S COMPANION

Zucchini is abundant and inexpensive during its peak months of June through late August. Select firm, unblemished zucchini. Smaller ones are tender and have bright flavor, while larger ones tend to be watery and seedy (those are best used in baked goods that benefit from their moisture). Store zucchini in a perforated plastic bag in the refrigerator crisper drawer for up to 3 days.

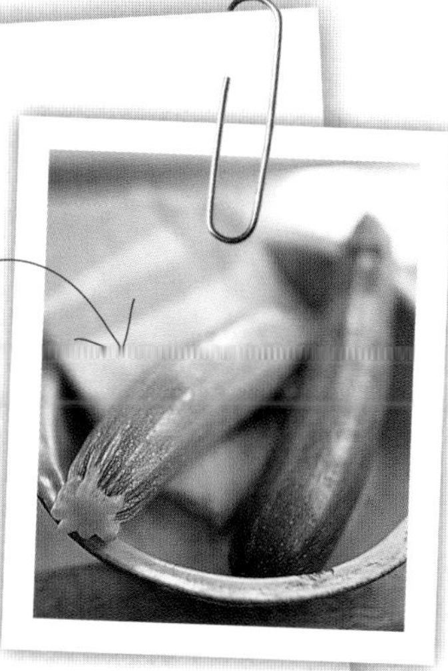

Easy Chicken and Dumplings

Deli-roasted chicken, cream of chicken soup, and canned biscuits make a quick-and-tasty version of this favorite.

MAKES 4 to 6 servings • **HANDS-ON TIME:** 30 min. • **TOTAL TIME:** 40 min.

- 1 (32-oz.) container low-sodium chicken broth
- 3 cups shredded cooked chicken (about 1½ lb.)
- 1 (10¾-oz.) can reduced-fat cream of chicken soup
- ¼ tsp. poultry seasoning
- 1 (10.2-oz.) can refrigerated jumbo buttermilk biscuits
- 2 carrots, diced
- 3 celery ribs, diced

1. Bring first 4 ingredients to a boil in a Dutch oven over medium-high heat. Cover, reduce heat to low, and simmer, stirring occasionally, 5 minutes. Increase heat to medium-high; return to a low boil.
2. Place biscuits on a lightly floured surface. Roll or pat each biscuit to ⅛-inch thickness; cut into ½-inch-wide strips.
3. Drop strips, 1 at a time, into boiling broth mixture. Add carrots and celery. Cover, reduce heat to low, and simmer 15 to 20 minutes, stirring occasionally to prevent dumplings from sticking.

One roasted chicken yields about 3 cups of meat.

Chicken-and-Sausage Gumbo

MAKES 4 to 6 servings • **HANDS-ON TIME:** 55 min. • **TOTAL TIME:** 3 hr., 55 min.

- 1 lb. andouille sausage, cut into ¼-inch-thick slices
- 4 skinned, bone-in chicken breasts
- Vegetable oil
- ¾ cup all-purpose flour
- 1 medium onion, chopped
- ½ green bell pepper, chopped
- 2 celery ribs, sliced
- 2 qt. hot water
- 3 garlic cloves, minced
- 2 bay leaves
- 1 Tbsp. Worcestershire sauce
- 2 tsp. Creole seasoning
- ½ tsp. dried thyme
- ½ to 1 tsp. hot sauce
- 4 green onions, sliced
- Filé powder (optional)
- Hot cooked rice
- Garnish: chopped green onions

1. Cook sausage in a Dutch oven over medium heat, stirring constantly, 5 minutes or until browned. Drain on paper towels, reserving drippings in Dutch oven. Set sausage aside.
2. Cook chicken in reserved drippings in Dutch oven over medium heat 5 minutes or until browned. Remove to paper towels, reserving drippings in Dutch oven. Set chicken aside.
3. Add enough oil to drippings in Dutch oven to measure ½ cup. Add flour, and cook over medium heat, stirring constantly, 20 to 25 minutes, or until roux is chocolate colored.
4. Stir in onion, bell pepper, and celery; cook, stirring often, 8 minutes or until tender. Gradually add 2 qt. hot water, and bring mixture to a boil; add chicken, garlic, and next 5 ingredients. Reduce heat to low, and simmer, stirring occasionally, 1 hour. Remove chicken; let cool.
5. Add sausage to gumbo; cook 30 minutes. Stir in sliced green onions; cook 30 more minutes.
6. Bone chicken, and cut meat into strips; return chicken to gumbo, and simmer 5 minutes. Remove and discard bay leaves.
7. Remove gumbo from heat. Sprinkle with filé powder, if desired. Serve over hot cooked rice. Garnish, if desired.

Beef Vegetable Soup

MAKES 18 cups • **HANDS-ON TIME:** 15 min. • **TOTAL TIME:** 1 hr., 15 min.

- 1½ lb. beef stew meat
- 1 Tbsp. olive oil
- 1 (32-oz.) bag frozen mixed vegetables (peas, carrots, green beans, and lima beans)
- 1 (15-oz.) can tomato sauce
- 1 (14.5-oz.) can Italian-style diced tomatoes
- 1 medium-size baking potato, peeled and diced
- 1 celery rib, chopped
- 1 medium onion, chopped
- 2 garlic cloves, minced
- ½ cup ketchup
- 1 extra-large chicken bouillon cube (we tested with Knorr)
- ½ tsp. pepper

1. Cook meat in hot oil over medium-high heat in a large Dutch oven 6 to 8 minutes or until browned.
2. Stir in frozen mixed vegetables, next 9 ingredients, and ½ qt. water, stirring to loosen particles from bottom of Dutch oven. Bring mixture to a boil over medium-high heat; cover, reduce heat to low, and simmer, stirring occasionally, 55 to 60 minutes or until potatoes are tender.

How To Sauté Stew Meat

When sautéing bite-size pieces of meat, stir frequently (but not constantly) to promote even browning and cooking. Portion-size cuts of meat should only be turned once so they have enough time to form a nice crust, which will also keep the meat from sticking to the pan.

Peppered Beef Soup

Freeze leftovers in an airtight container up to 3 months. Add a bit of canned broth when reheating to reach desired consistency.

make ahead

MAKES 12 cups • **HANDS-ON TIME:** 20 min. • **TOTAL TIME:** 8 hr., 28 min.

- 1 (4-lb.) sirloin tip beef roast
- ½ cup all-purpose flour
- 2 Tbsp. canola oil
- 1 medium-size red onion, thinly sliced
- 6 garlic cloves, minced
- 2 large baking potatoes, peeled and diced
- 1 (16-oz.) package baby carrots
- 2 (12-oz.) bottles lager beer*
- 2 Tbsp. balsamic vinegar
- 2 Tbsp. Worcestershire sauce
- 2 Tbsp. dried parsley flakes
- 1 Tbsp. beef bouillon granules
- 1½ to 3 tsp. freshly ground pepper
- 4 bay leaves
- Salt to taste

1. Rinse roast, and pat dry. Cut a 1-inch-deep cavity in the shape of an "X" on top of roast. (Do not cut all the way through roast.) Dredge roast in all-purpose flour; shake off excess.
2. Cook roast in hot oil in a Dutch oven over medium-high heat 1 to 2 minutes on each side or until lightly browned.
3. Place roast in a 6-qt. slow cooker. Stuff cavity with sliced red onion and minced garlic; top roast with potatoes and baby carrots. Pour beer, balsamic vinegar, and Worcestershire sauce into slow cooker. Sprinkle with parsley, bouillon granules, and ground pepper. Add bay leaves to liquid in slow cooker.
4. Cover and cook on LOW 7 to 8 hours or until fork-tender. Remove and discard bay leaves. Shred roast using 2 forks. Season with salt to taste.
*3 cups low-sodium beef broth may be substituted.

Harvest Lamb Stew

MAKES 8 servings • **HANDS-ON TIME:** 20 min. • **TOTAL TIME:** 5 hr., 11 min.

- 2½ lb. lean lamb stew meat (about 1-inch pieces)
- 1½ tsp. salt
- ¼ tsp. freshly ground pepper
- ¼ cup all-purpose flour
- 4 Tbsp. olive oil
- 1 (6-oz.) can tomato paste
- 1 (14.5-oz.) can beef broth
- 1 cup chopped celery
- 1 cup chopped sweet onion
- 3 garlic cloves, crushed
- 1 small butternut squash (about 1 lb.), peeled, seeded, and chopped
- Hot cooked mashed potatoes (optional)
- Garnish: fresh parsley sprigs

1. Rinse lamb stew meat, and pat dry. Sprinkle with salt and pepper; toss in flour, shaking off excess.
2. Cook half of lamb in 2 Tbsp. hot oil in a Dutch oven over medium-high heat, stirring occasionally, 10 minutes or until browned. Repeat procedure with remaining lamb and oil. Stir in tomato paste; cook 1 minute. Add broth, and stir to loosen particles from bottom of Dutch oven. Transfer mixture to a 6-qt. slow cooker.
3. Stir in celery, onion, and garlic. Top with butternut squash. (Do not stir to incorporate.) Cover and cook on LOW 4½ hours or until meat is tender. Serve over hot cooked mashed potatoes, if desired. Garnish, if desired.

Harvest Beef Stew: Substitute 2½ lb. beef stew meat for lamb. Proceed with recipe as directed.

How To Peel and Cut Butternut Squash

Use a sharp kitchen knife to cut 1 inch from the top and bottom of the squash, and discard. Using a serrated peeler, peel away the thick skin until you reach the deeper orange flesh of the squash. With a spoon or melon baller, scoop away the seeds and membranes; discard.

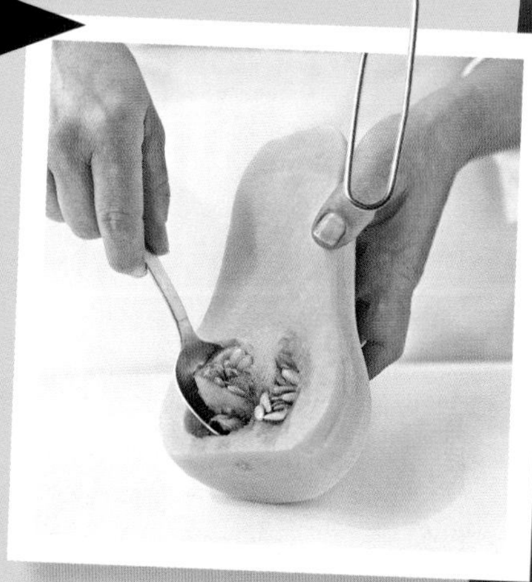

Quick Turkey Chili

MAKES 6 to 8 servings • **HANDS-ON TIME:** 15 min. • **TOTAL TIME:** 1 hr.

- 1 medium onion, chopped
- 1 Tbsp. vegetable oil
- 2 garlic cloves, chopped
- 1 lb. ground turkey
- 2 Tbsp. chili powder
- 2 tsp. ground cumin
- 3 Tbsp. tomato paste
- 1 (28-oz.) can diced tomatoes
- 1 (16-oz.) can red kidney beans, drained and rinsed
- 1 cup chicken broth
- 1 cup beer*
- 1 tsp. salt
- ½ tsp. pepper
- ¼ cup chopped fresh cilantro
- Garnish: sour cream

1. Sauté chopped onion in hot oil in a large Dutch oven over medium-high heat 5 minutes or until tender; add garlic, and sauté 1 minute.
2. Add turkey, chili powder, and cumin, and cook, stirring often, 8 minutes or until meat crumbles and is no longer pink. Stir in tomato paste, and cook 2 minutes. Add tomatoes and next 5 ingredients. Bring mixture to a boil; cover, reduce heat to low, and simmer, stirring occasionally, 30 minutes. Stir in cilantro. Garnish, if desired.
*Chicken broth may be substituted.

Don't let the long list of ingredients deter you; chances are you'll have most of them on hand.

Black Bean Chili

MAKES 8 servings • **HANDS-ON TIME:** 10 min. • **TOTAL TIME:** 30 min.

- 3 (15-oz.) cans black beans
- 1 large sweet onion, chopped
- 1 (12-oz.) package meatless burger crumbles (we tested with Boca)
- 2 Tbsp. vegetable oil
- 4 tsp. chili powder
- 1 tsp. ground cumin
- ½ tsp. pepper
- ¼ tsp. salt
- 1 (14-oz.) can low-sodium fat-free chicken broth
- 2 (14.5-oz.) cans petite diced tomatoes with jalapeños

Toppings: sour cream, shredded Cheddar cheese, lime wedges, sliced jalapeño peppers, chopped fresh cilantro, chopped tomatoes, corn chips

1. Drain and rinse 2 cans black beans. (Do not drain third can.)
2. Sauté chopped onion and burger crumbles in hot oil in a large Dutch oven over medium heat 6 minutes. Stir in chili powder and next 3 ingredients; sauté 1 minute. Stir in drained and undrained beans, chicken broth, and diced tomatoes. Bring to a boil over medium-high heat; cover, reduce heat to low, and simmer 10 minutes. Serve chili with desired toppings.

Meaty Black Bean Chili: Substitute 1 lb. ground round for meatless burger crumbles, sautéing ground round with onion 10 minutes or until meat is no longer pink. Omit vegetable oil. Proceed as directed.

Meatless Chili

This chili also works as a burrito filling. Just spoon some chili onto a warm flour tortilla, sprinkle with shredded lettuce and cheese, and roll up the tortilla.

healthy & hearty

MAKES 4 servings • **HANDS-ON TIME:** 5 min. • **TOTAL TIME:** 18 min.

- Cooking spray
- 2 tsp. jarred minced garlic
- 1 large onion, chopped
- 1 (16-oz.) can chili-hot beans, undrained
- 1 (14.5-oz.) can no-salt-added diced tomatoes, undrained
- 1 tsp. chili powder
- 1 tsp. ground cumin
- 12 oz. frozen vegetable and grain protein crumbles (about 3 cups)

Topping: oyster crackers

1. Coat a 4-qt. saucepan with cooking spray. Place pan over medium-high heat. Add garlic and onion; sauté 3 minutes. Add beans and next 3 ingredients. Bring to a boil, stirring occasionally; reduce heat, and simmer 5 minutes. Add protein crumbles, and cook 3 minutes or until thoroughly heated. Top with oyster crackers, if desired.

Meatless Chili

Tuscan Beef and Bread Salad

MAKES 6 servings • **HANDS-ON TIME:** 25 min. • **TOTAL TIME:** 35 min.

- 8 (½-inch-thick) Italian bread slices
- 2 medium-size sweet onions, cut into ¼-inch rounds
- 6 Tbsp. light balsamic vinaigrette, divided
- ¾ tsp. salt, divided
- ¾ tsp. freshly ground pepper, divided
- 3 (¾-inch-thick) top sirloin steaks (about 1½ lb.)
- 6 medium-size plum tomatoes, chopped (about 3½ cups)
- ⅓ cup chopped fresh basil
- ¼ cup freshly shaved Parmesan cheese
- Garnishes: fresh basil leaves, cracked pepper

1. Preheat a charcoal grill to medium, ash-covered coals, or a gas grill to 300° to 350° (medium) heat. Brush 1 side of bread and onion with 2 Tbsp. vinaigrette. Sprinkle onion with ¼ tsp. salt and ¼ tsp. pepper.
2. Grill steaks and onion at the same time. Grill steaks on a charcoal grill, without grill lid, 10 to 12 minutes, or on a gas grill, covered with grill lid, 7 to 10 minutes. Grill onion, on 1 side only, on a charcoal grill, without grill lid, 8 minutes or until tender and grill marks appear, or on a gas grill, covered with grill lid, 6 minutes or until tender and grill marks appear.
3. Remove steaks and onion from grill. Sprinkle steaks with remaining ½ tsp. salt and ½ tsp. pepper. Let steaks stand 5 minutes.
4. Meanwhile, grill bread on a charcoal grill, without grill lid, 1 to 2 minutes on each side or until lightly browned and grill marks appear, or on a gas grill, covered with grill lid, 1 to 2 minutes on each side or until lightly browned and grill marks appear.
5. Cut steaks into thin strips. Cut strips into bite-size pieces. Coarsely chop onion. Cut bread into 1-inch cubes.
6. Toss steak pieces, onion, bread, tomatoes, and chopped basil with remaining 4 Tbsp. vinaigrette. Season with salt and pepper to taste. Sprinkle with cheese. Let stand 5 minutes before serving. Garnish, if desired.

Tex-Mex Beef-and-Beans Chopped Salad

Find refrigerated salsa in your grocer's produce or deli area. We prefer it in this recipe for chunky texture and fresh flavor. This recipe is also great with pulled pork.

30-minute special

MAKES 6 servings • **HANDS-ON TIME:** 25 min. • **TOTAL TIME:** 25 min.

- **¾ cup bottled Ranch dressing**
- **¾ cup refrigerated salsa**
- **1 (22-oz.) package romaine lettuce hearts, chopped**
- **1 (15-oz.) can black beans, drained and rinsed**
- **3 cups crushed tortilla chips**
- **6 oz. pepper Jack cheese, cut into small cubes**
- **1 cup seeded and chopped cucumber**
- **1 cup diced jícama**
- **3 plum tomatoes, seeded and chopped**
- **1 medium avocado, chopped**
- **¾ lb. barbecued beef brisket (without sauce), chopped and warmed***

1. Stir together ¾ cup Ranch dressing and salsa.

2. Toss together romaine and next 7 ingredients. Drizzle with dressing mixture, and top with brisket. Serve immediately.

*Grilled flank steak, chopped, may be substituted.

How To Seed a Tomato

Seeding tomatoes gets rid of excess liquid and the bitter seeds that can sometimes alter a dish's flavor. Cut the tomato in half horizontally. Using a spoon, scoop the seeds and pulp away from the flesh, and discard. Or, cup the tomato half in the palm of your hand, and gently squeeze out the seeds. Either way, you're left with 2 clean tomato halves.

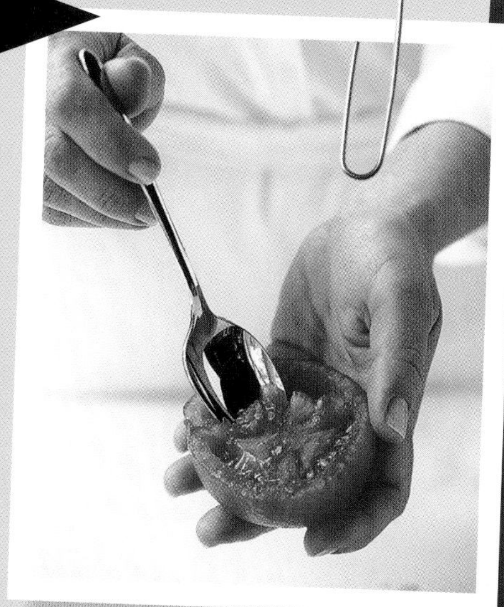

Spicy Pork-and-Orange Chopped Salad

Combining romaine and coleslaw mix makes this dish crispy and crunchy.

MAKES 4 servings • **HANDS-ON TIME:** 28 min. • **TOTAL TIME:** 33 min.

- **1 lb. pork tenderloin, cut into ½-inch pieces**
- **2½ tsp. Szechwan seasoning blend (we tested with McCormick Gourmet Collection)**
- **½ tsp. salt**
- **1 Tbsp. olive oil**
- **2 oranges**
- **½ cup bottled low-fat sesame-ginger dressing**
- **1 cup seeded and chopped cucumber**
- **¼ cup chopped fresh cilantro**
- **1 romaine lettuce heart, chopped**
- **3 cups shredded coleslaw mix**
- **½ cup wasabi-and-soy sauce-flavored almonds (we tested with Blue Diamond)**

1. Toss pork with Szechwan seasoning and salt to coat. Sauté pork in hot oil in a large nonstick skillet over medium-high heat 8 to 10 minutes or until done.
2. Peel oranges, and cut into ½-inch-thick slices. Cut slices into chunks.
3. Pour dressing into a salad bowl. Stir in oranges, cucumber, and cilantro. Let stand 5 minutes. Add romaine, coleslaw mix, and pork; toss gently. Sprinkle with almonds. Serve immediately.

Pork Tenderloin and Tomato Salad

Save the crumbled bacon from the dressing to scatter over the salad.

MAKES 4 servings • **HANDS-ON TIME:** 35 min. • **TOTAL TIME:** 1 hr., 24 min., including vinaigrette

- 1 (1-lb.) pork tenderloin
- 1 Tbsp. coarsely ground pepper
- ¾ tsp. salt
- 2 Tbsp. olive oil
- 1 (5-oz.) package spring mix
- 3 large tomatoes, cut into ½-inch slices
- Warm Bacon Vinaigrette
- Garnish: cooked and crumbled bacon

1. Preheat oven to 400°. Remove silver skin from tenderloin, leaving a thin layer of fat.
2. Rub pepper and salt over pork. Cook pork in hot oil in a large skillet over medium-high heat 5 minutes on all sides or until browned. Transfer to a 13- x 9-inch pan.
3. Bake at 400° for 15 minutes or until a meat thermometer inserted into thickest portion registers 155°. Let stand 10 to 12 minutes or until thermometer registers 160°.
4. Cut pork into ¼-inch-thick slices. Divide greens among 4 plates; arrange tomato slices and pork over greens. Serve immediately with Warm Bacon Vinaigrette. Garnish, if desired.

Warm Bacon Vinaigrette

MAKES about 1½ cups • **HANDS-ON TIME:** 22 min. • **TOTAL TIME:** 22 min.

- 4 bacon slices
- 4 Tbsp. minced shallots
- 2 Tbsp. minced garlic
- 3 Tbsp. brown sugar
- 6 Tbsp. orange juice
- 5 Tbsp. balsamic vinegar
- [illegible] Tbsp. coarse grained mustard
- ⅓ cup olive oil
- ½ tsp. salt

1. Cook bacon in a large skillet over medium-high heat 8 to 10 minutes or until crisp; remove bacon, and drain on paper towels, reserving 2 Tbsp. drippings in skillet. Crumble bacon, and reserve for another use.
2. Cook shallots and garlic in hot drippings over medium heat, stirring occasionally, 3 minutes or until tender. Add brown sugar, and cook, stirring constantly, 1 minute or until sugar is dissolved.
3. Process garlic mixture, orange juice, and next 4 ingredients in a blender until combined.

Picnic Salad with Honey-Mustard Dressing

The chicken marinates in as little as 4 hours, but it's best when started the night before. If you want to serve 4 people, this recipe easily doubles, but you'll need to fry the chicken in 2 batches.

MAKES 2 servings • **HANDS-ON TIME:** 29 min. • **TOTAL TIME:** 4 hr., 29 min., including dressing

- 2 skinned and boned chicken breasts (about 1 lb.)
- ¼ cup thinly sliced fresh basil
- 2 cups mayonnaise
- ½ cup milk
- 2 tsp. minced garlic
- 4 tsp. freshly ground black pepper, divided
- 2 tsp. salt, divided
- 8 thick-cut bacon slices
- 2 cups vegetable oil
- 2 cups all-purpose flour
- 1 head green leaf lettuce, chopped
- 2 cups seeded and cubed watermelon, cantaloupe, or honeydew melon
- Honey-Mustard Dressing
- Garnish: fresh basil sprigs

1. Butterfly chicken breasts by making a lengthwise cut horizontally through breasts to within ½ inch of other side. Open breasts, and sprinkle evenly with sliced basil; place between 2 sheets of heavy-duty plastic wrap. Flatten chicken to ½-inch thickness, using a rolling pin or the flat side of a meat mallet.
2. Stir together mayonnaise, milk, garlic, 2 tsp. pepper, and 1 tsp. salt in a shallow dish; add chicken. Cover and chill at least 4 hours or up to 24 hours.
3. Cook bacon slices in a large cast-iron skillet until crisp; remove bacon, and drain on paper towels, reserving drippings in skillet. Crumble bacon, and set aside. Add oil to drippings in skillet, and heat to 350°, stirring to loosen particles from bottom of skillet.
4. Combine flour, remaining 2 tsp. black pepper, and remaining 1 tsp. salt in a shallow dish. Remove chicken from marinade, discarding marinade. Scrape and discard excess marinade from chicken. Dredge chicken in flour mixture. Fry 2 to 3 minutes on each side or until golden brown and chicken is done.
5. Divide lettuce evenly between each of 2 serving plates. Top each with 1 cup melon, and drizzle with desired amount of Honey-Mustard Dressing. Cut chicken into thin slices, and place evenly on top of melon. Sprinkle with bacon, and garnish, if desired. Serve immediately.

Honey-Mustard Dressing

MAKES 1¾ servings • **HANDS-ON TIME:** 10 min. • **TOTAL TIME:** 4 hr., 10 min.

You can prepare this dressing up to 2 days ahead of time or the morning before you serve it.

- 1 cup mayonnaise
- 3 Tbsp. yellow mustard
- 3 Tbsp. honey
- 2 Tbsp. chopped fresh basil
- 2 Tbsp. vegetable oil
- 2 tsp. cider vinegar
- ½ tsp. minced garlic
- ¼ tsp. ground red pepper

1. Whisk together all ingredients; cover and chill at least 4 hours.

Chicken and Wild Rice Salad

MAKES 6 servings • **HANDS-ON TIME:** 10 min. • **TOTAL TIME:** 25 min.

- 1 cup chopped pecans
- 3 Tbsp. soy sauce
- 3 Tbsp. rice wine vinegar
- 2 Tbsp. sesame oil
- 1 (8.5-oz.) pouch ready-to-serve whole grain brown and wild rice mix
- 3 cups shredded cooked chicken
- 1 cup diced red bell pepper
- 1 cup coarsely chopped watercress
- ¼ cup minced green onions
- Black pepper to taste

1. Preheat oven to 350°. Bake pecans in a single layer in a shallow pan 10 to 12 minutes or until toasted and fragrant, stirring halfway through.
2. Whisk together soy sauce, vinegar, and sesame oil in a large bowl.
3. Prepare brown and wild rice mix according to package directions. Stir chicken, next 3 ingredients, toasted pecans, and rice into soy sauce mixture. Add black pepper to taste.

Muffaletta Pasta Salad

MAKES 5 servings • **HANDS-ON TIME:** 15 min. • **TOTAL TIME:** 15 min.

- **1 (19-oz.) package frozen cheese tortellini**
- **½ (9-oz.) package ham, cut into bite-size pieces**
- **½ (7-oz.) package salami, cut into bite-size pieces**
- **1 cup olive salad, drained**
- **½ cup olive oil vinaigrette**
- **2 Tbsp. chopped fresh parsley**
- **½ tsp. freshly ground pepper**
- **Garnish: fresh parsley sprigs**

1. Prepare tortellini according to package directions.
2. Toss together tortellini, ham, and next 5 ingredients. Serve immediately, or cover and chill 2 to 8 hours. Garnish, if desired.

Farfalle Garden Pasta Salad

MAKES 8 servings • **HANDS-ON TIME:** 20 min. • **TOTAL TIME:** 2 hr., 40 min.

- **1 (16-oz.) box farfalle (bow-tie) pasta**
- **½ cup extra virgin olive oil, divided**
- **½ cup red wine vinegar**
- **1 tsp. lemon zest**
- **1 tsp. Dijon mustard**
- **Salt and pepper to taste**
- **½ lb. fresh green beans, cut into 1-inch pieces**
- **1 medium zucchini, diced**
- **2 medium carrots, diced**
- **1 pt. cherry tomatoes, cut in half**
- **1 (4-oz.) package crumbled feta cheese**
- **2 green onions, sliced (white part only)**
- **1 Tbsp. chopped fresh oregano**
- **1 Tbsp. chopped fresh mint**

1. Cook pasta according to package directions. Drain well, and spread onto a baking sheet. Drizzle with 1 Tbsp. oil, tossing to coat. Let stand at least 5 minutes. Transfer pasta to a bowl.
2. Whisk together vinegar, lemon zest, and mustard in a small bowl; gradually add remaining olive oil in a slow, steady stream, whisking until blended. Whisk in salt and pepper to taste.
3. Cook green beans, zucchini, and carrots in boiling salted water to cover 3 minutes or until crisp-tender; drain.
4. Toss together pasta, vinegar mixture, cooked vegetables, tomatoes, and remaining ingredients in a large bowl until combined. Cover and chill at least 2 hours.

Farfalle Garden Pasta Salad

Summer Tortellini Salad

Summer Tortellini Salad

MAKES 4 servings • **HANDS-ON TIME:** 20 min. • **TOTAL TIME:** 45 min.

- 1 (19-oz.) package frozen cheese tortellini (we tested with Rosetto Cheese)
- 2 cups chopped cooked chicken
- ¼ cup sliced green olives
- ¼ cup sliced black olives
- ¼ cup diced red bell pepper
- 2 Tbsp. chopped sweet onion
- 2 Tbsp. chopped fresh parsley
- 2 Tbsp. mayonnaise
- 1 Tbsp. red wine vinegar
- 1 tsp. herbes de Provence*
- ¼ cup canola oil
- Salt to taste
- Garnish: fresh parsley sprigs

1. Cook tortellini according to package directions; drain. Plunge into ice water to stop the cooking process; drain and place in a large bowl. Stir in chicken and next 5 ingredients.
2. Whisk together mayonnaise, red wine vinegar, and herbes de Provence. Add oil in a slow, steady stream, whisking constantly until smooth. Pour over tortellini mixture, tossing to coat. Stir in salt to taste. Cover and chill at least 25 minutes. Garnish, if desired.
*1 tsp. dried Italian seasoning may be substituted.

Tuna Tortellini Salad: Substitute 1 (12-oz.) can albacore tuna, drained well and rinsed, for chicken. Prepare recipe as directed.

Tortellini Salad

MAKES 4 servings • **HANDS-ON TIME:** 10 min. • **TOTAL TIME:** 10 min.

- 2 (9-oz.) packages refrigerated cheese tortellini
- 1 (14-oz.) can quartered artichoke hearts, drained
- 1 cup Caesar salad dressing
- 3 oz. salami, sliced
- 1 (2¼-oz.) can sliced black olives, drained
- 4 green onions, chopped
- Garnish: whole green onions

1. Cook cheese tortellini according to package directions; drain and rinse with cold water.
2. Toss together tortellini and next 5 ingredients; garnish, if desired. Serve immediately.

Zesty Chicken-Pasta Salad

MAKES 4 servings • **HANDS-ON TIME:** 15 min. • **TOTAL TIME:** 1 hr., 15 min.

- 1 (8-oz.) package elbow macaroni
- 1 (13-oz.) bottle peppercorn-Ranch dressing
- 2½ cups chopped cooked chicken
- 1 (9-oz.) package frozen sweet peas, thawed
- 1 (2¼-oz.) can sliced black olives, drained
- 1 pt. cherry tomatoes, halved
- Salt to taste

1. Cook elbow macaroni according to package directions; drain and rinse with cold water. Stir together macaroni and remaining ingredients; chill at least 1 hour.

Porcini Mushroom Tortelloni with Wilted Greens

MAKES 4 servings • **HANDS-ON TIME:** 32 min. • **TOTAL TIME:** 32 min.

- 1 (8-oz.) package porcini mushroom tortelloni (we tested with Barilla)
- 4 bacon slices, chopped
- 1 small onion, chopped
- 1 garlic clove, minced
- ¼ cup dry white wine
- 1 to 2 Tbsp. balsamic vinegar
- ½ cup chicken broth
- ½ cup frozen green peas
- 2 plum tomatoes, chopped
- ½ (5.5-oz.) package baby spinach-and-spring greens mix (we tested with Fresh Express 50/50 Mix)
- ½ cup freshly shaved Parmesan cheese

1. Prepare tortelloni according to package directions. Keep warm.
2. Meanwhile, cook bacon in a large skillet over medium-high heat 6 to 8 minutes or until crisp; remove bacon, reserving 2 Tbsp. drippings in skillet. Add onion, and sauté 3 minutes or until tender. Stir in garlic, and sauté 1 minute. Stir in wine and vinegar, and cook 2 minutes, stirring to loosen particles from bottom of skillet.
3. Stir in chicken broth, peas, tomatoes, and tortelloni, and cook 2 to 3 minutes or until thoroughly heated. Serve over salad greens, and sprinkle evenly with Parmesan cheese.

Porcini Mushroom Tortelloni with Wilted Greens

Shrimp-and-Pasta Salad

Light and lemony, this recipe easily doubles for dinner with friends.

MAKES 4 servings • **HANDS-ON TIME:** 20 min. • **TOTAL TIME:** 20 min., including dressing

- 8 oz. uncooked medium-size shell pasta
- Lemon-Herb Dressing with Mint and Tarragon
- 1 lb. peeled, medium-size cooked shrimp
- 1 large nectarine, cut into thin wedges
- 1 cup chopped seedless cucumber
- Garnishes: fresh raspberries, arugula

1. Cook pasta according to package directions; drain. Plunge into ice water to stop the cooking process; drain and place in a large bowl. Add ½ cup dressing, tossing to coat. Stir in shrimp, nectarine, and cucumber. Serve with remaining ¼ cup dressing. Garnish, if desired.

Lemon-Herb Dressing with Mint and Tarragon

MAKES ¾ cups • **HANDS-ON TIME:** 10 min. • **TOTAL TIME:** 10 min.

- ⅓ cup canola oil
- 3 Tbsp. chopped fresh mint
- 1 Tbsp. chopped fresh tarragon
- 1 Tbsp. honey mustard
- 1 tsp. lemon zest
- ¼ cup fresh lemon juice
- 1 tsp. salt
- ½ tsp. dried crushed red pepper

1. Whisk together all ingredients until blended.

Lemon-Herb Dressing with Chives and Tarragon: Substitute chopped fresh chives for mint. Proceed with recipe as directed.

Lemon-Herb Dressing with Basil: Substitute ⅓ cup chopped fresh basil for mint and tarragon. Proceed with recipe as directed. Season with salt to taste.

casseroles
AND
dutch
oven
dinners

Classic Baked Macaroni and Cheese

Whisk warm milk into the flour mixture to ensure a lump-free sauce. We also recommend shredding your own cheese for a creamier texture.

MAKES 6 to 8 servings • **HANDS-ON TIME:** 22 min. • **TOTAL TIME:** 47 min.

- 2 cups milk
- 2 Tbsp. butter
- 2 Tbsp. all-purpose flour
- ½ tsp. salt
- ¼ tsp. freshly ground black pepper
- 1 (10-oz.) block extra-sharp Cheddar cheese, shredded (we tested with Cracker Barrel Extra-Sharp Cheddar)
- ¼ tsp. ground red pepper (optional)
- ½ (16-oz.) package elbow macaroni, cooked

1. Preheat oven to 400°. Microwave milk at HIGH 1½ minutes. Melt butter in a large skillet or Dutch oven over medium-low heat; whisk in flour until smooth. Cook, whisking constantly, 1 minute.
2. Gradually whisk in warm milk, and cook, whisking constantly, 5 minutes or until thickened.
3. Whisk in salt, black pepper, 1 cup shredded cheese, and, if desired, red pepper until smooth; stir in pasta. Spoon pasta mixture into a lightly greased 2-qt. baking dish; top with remaining cheese. Bake at 400° for 20 minutes or until golden and bubbly.

Three-Cheese Baked Pasta

Prepare up to 1 day ahead; cover and refrigerate. Let stand at room temperature 30 minutes, and bake as directed. Ziti pasta is shaped in long, thin tubes; penne or rigatoni pasta may be substituted.

make ahead

MAKES 8 to 10 servings • **HANDS-ON TIME:** 10 min. • **TOTAL TIME:** 50 min.

- 1 (16-oz.) package ziti pasta
- 2 (10-oz.) containers Alfredo sauce (we tested with refrigerated Buitoni)
- 1 (8-oz.) container sour cream
- 1 (15-oz.) container ricotta cheese
- 2 large eggs, lightly beaten
- ¼ cup grated Parmesan cheese
- ¼ cup chopped fresh parsley
- 1½ cups (6 oz.) mozzarella cheese

1. Preheat oven to 350°. Cook ziti according to package directions; drain and return to pot.
2. Stir together Alfredo sauce and sour cream; toss with ziti until evenly coated. Spoon half of ziti mixture into a lightly greased 13- x 9-inch baking dish.
3. Stir together ricotta cheese and next 3 ingredients; spread evenly over pasta mixture. Spoon remaining pasta mixture evenly over ricotta cheese layer; sprinkle with mozzarella cheese.
4. Bake at 350° for 30 minutes or until bubbly.

Three-Cheese Baked Pasta

Spinach-Ravioli Lasagna

Although this dish calls for frozen ravioli, you can let the ravioli sit on the countertop for about 5 minutes before preparing the recipe to allow the frozen ravioli to separate more easily.

MAKES 6 to 8 servings • **HANDS-ON TIME:** 10 min. • **TOTAL TIME:** 45 min.

- 1 (6-oz.) package fresh baby spinach
- ⅓ cup pesto sauce
- 1 (15-oz.) jar Alfredo sauce (we tested with Bertolli)
- ¼ cup vegetable broth*
- 1 (25-oz.) package frozen cheese-filled ravioli (do not thaw)
- 1 cup (4 oz.) shredded Italian six-cheese blend
- Garnishes: chopped fresh basil, paprika

1. Preheat oven to 375°. Chop spinach, and toss with pesto in a medium bowl.
2. Combine Alfredo sauce and vegetable broth. Spoon one-third of Alfredo sauce mixture (about ½ cup) into a lightly greased 2.2-qt. or 11- x 7-inch baking dish. Top with half of spinach mixture. Arrange half of ravioli in a single layer over spinach mixture. Repeat layers once. Top with remaining Alfredo sauce.
3. Bake at 375° for 30 minutes. Remove from oven, and sprinkle with shredded cheese. Bake 5 minutes or until hot and bubbly. Garnish, if desired.
*Chicken broth may be substituted.

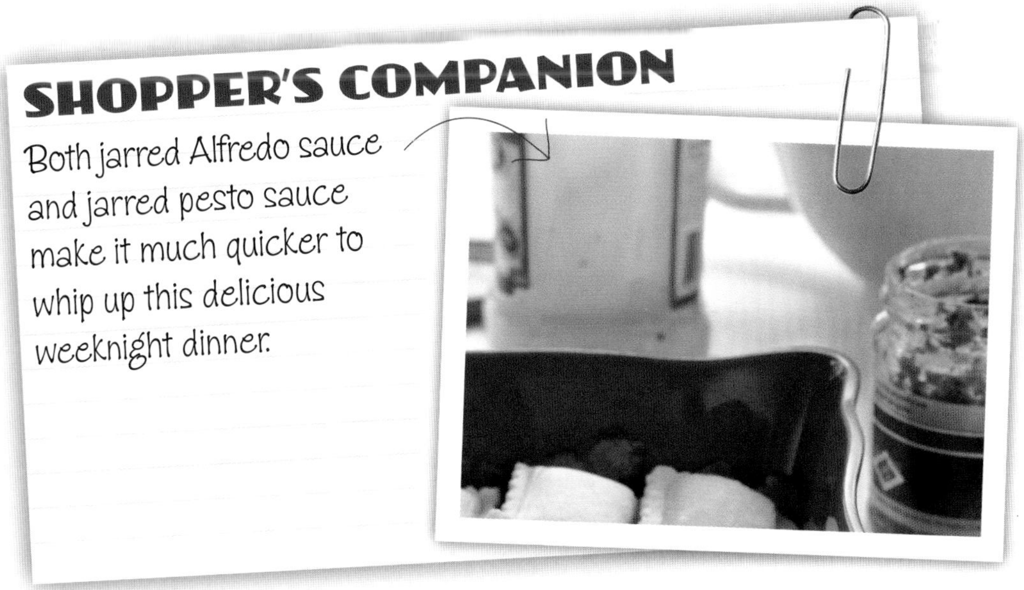

Eggplant Parmesan Lasagna

MAKES 8 to 10 servings • **HANDS-ON TIME:** 50 min. • **TOTAL TIME:** 1 hr., 50 min.

- 2 (26-oz.) jars tomato, garlic, and onion pasta sauce (we tested with Bertolli)
- ¼ cup chopped fresh basil
- ½ tsp. dried crushed red pepper
- ½ cup whipping cream
- 1 cup grated Parmesan cheese
- 1 large eggplant (about 1½ lb.)
- ½ tsp. salt
- ¼ tsp. black pepper
- 3 large eggs, lightly beaten
- 1 cup all-purpose flour
- 6 Tbsp. olive oil
- 6 lasagna noodles, cooked and drained
- 1 (15-oz.) container part-skim ricotta cheese
- 2 cups (8 oz.) shredded mozzarella cheese

1. Preheat oven to 350°. Cook first 3 ingredients in a 3½-qt. saucepan over medium-low heat 30 minutes. Remove from heat; stir in cream and Parmesan cheese. Set aside.
2. Peel eggplant, and cut crosswise into ¼-inch-thick slices. Sprinkle slices evenly with salt and black pepper. Stir together eggs and 3 Tbsp. water. Dredge eggplant in flour; dip into egg mixture, and dredge again in flour, shaking to remove excess.
3. Cook eggplant, in batches, in 1½ Tbsp. hot oil in a large nonstick skillet over medium-high heat 4 minutes on each side or until golden brown and slightly softened. Drain on paper towels. Repeat with remaining oil and eggplant, wiping skillet clean after each batch, if necessary.
4. Layer 3 lasagna noodles lengthwise in a lightly greased 13- x 9-inch baking dish. Top with one-third of tomato sauce mixture and half of eggplant. Dollop half of ricotta cheese evenly on eggplant in dish; top with half of mozzarella. Repeat layers with remaining noodles, one-third of sauce mixture, remaining eggplant, and remaining ricotta. Top with remaining one-third of sauce mixture and mozzarella cheese.
5. Bake at 350° for 35 to 40 minutes or until golden brown. Let stand 20 minutes before serving.

SHORTCUT SECRET

Substitute 6 no-cook lasagna noodles for the cooked lasagna noodles. Prepare recipe as directed, reserving last half of mozzarella for top. Bake, covered, at 350° for 45 minutes. Sprinkle top with reserved cheese; bake, uncovered, for 20 more minutes or until golden brown.

Classic Chicken Tetrazzini

MAKES 8 to 10 servings • **HANDS-ON TIME:** 20 min. • **TOTAL TIME:** 55 min.

- 1½ (8-oz.) packages vermicelli
- ½ cup butter
- ½ cup all-purpose flour
- 4 cups milk
- ½ cup dry white wine
- 2 Tbsp. chicken bouillon granules
- 1 tsp. seasoned pepper
- 2 cups freshly grated Parmesan cheese, divided
- 4 cups diced cooked chicken
- 1 (6-oz.) jar sliced mushrooms, drained
- ¾ cup slivered almonds

1. Preheat oven to 350°. Prepare pasta according to package directions.
2. Meanwhile, melt butter in a Dutch oven over low heat; whisk in flour until smooth. Cook 1 minute, whisking constantly. Gradually whisk in milk and wine; cook over medium heat, whisking constantly, 8 to 10 minutes or until mixture is thickened and bubbly. Whisk in bouillon granules, seasoned pepper, and 1 cup Parmesan cheese.
3. Remove from heat; stir in diced cooked chicken, sliced mushrooms, and hot cooked pasta.
4. Spoon mixture into a lightly greased 13- x 9-inch baking dish; sprinkle with slivered almonds and remaining 1 cup Parmesan cheese.
5. Bake at 350° for 35 minutes or until bubbly.

SHORTCUT SECRET

A speedy Italian classic, Chicken Tetrazzini can be made ahead for easy weeknight dinners. Freeze an unbaked casserole up to 1 month, if desired. Thaw overnight in refrigerator. Let stand 30 minutes at room temperature, and bake as directed.

Chicken-and-Rice Casserole

Use a rotisserie chicken for this family-friendly casserole. The potato chip topping promises to be a hit.

make ahead

MAKES 8 servings • **HANDS-ON TIME:** 20 min. • **TOTAL TIME:** 40 min.

- 2 Tbsp. butter
- 1 medium onion, chopped
- 1 (8.8-oz.) package microwaveable rice of choice
- 3 cups chopped cooked chicken
- 1½ cups frozen petite peas
- 1½ cups (6 oz.) shredded sharp Cheddar cheese
- 1 cup mayonnaise
- 1 (10¾-oz.) can cream of chicken soup
- 1 (8-oz.) can sliced water chestnuts, drained
- 1 (4-oz.) jar sliced pimientos, drained
- 3 cups coarsely crushed ridged potato chips

1. Preheat oven to 350°. Melt butter in a skillet over medium heat. Add onion, and sauté 5 minutes or until tender.
2. Cook rice in microwave according to package directions. Combine sautéed onion, rice, chicken, and next 6 ingredients in a large bowl; toss gently. Spoon mixture into a lightly greased 13- x 9-inch baking dish. Top with coarsely crushed potato chips.
3. Bake, uncovered, at 350° for 20 to 25 minutes or until bubbly.

SHORTCUT SECRET

To make this casserole ahead, prepare and spoon the casserole into the baking dish, leaving off crushed chips. Cover and refrigerate up to 24 hours. Uncover and add crushed chips before baking.

Leslie's Favorite Chicken-and-Wild Rice Casserole

This is one of those creamy, cheesy chicken casseroles. Perfect for a big family get-together, it feeds a crowd. You can make and freeze the casserole ahead, or make 2 smaller casseroles.

MAKES 10 to 12 servings • **HANDS-ON TIME:** 40 min. • **TOTAL TIME:** 1 hr., 20 min.

make ahead

- **2 (6.2-oz.) packages fast-cooking long-grain and wild rice mix**
- **¼ cup butter**
- **4 celery ribs, chopped**
- **2 medium onions, chopped**
- **2 (8-oz.) cans sliced water chestnuts, drained**
- **5 cups chopped cooked chicken**
- **4 cups (16 oz.) shredded Cheddar cheese, divided**
- **2 (10¾-oz.) cans cream of mushroom soup**
- **2 (8-oz.) containers sour cream**
- **1 cup milk**
- **½ tsp. salt**
- **½ tsp. pepper**
- **2 cups soft breadcrumbs (homemade)**
- **1 (2.25-oz.) package sliced almonds, toasted**

1. Preheat oven to 350°. Prepare rice mixes according to package directions.
2. Meanwhile, melt butter in a large skillet over medium heat; add celery and onions. Sauté 10 minutes or until tender. Stir in rice, water chestnuts, chicken, 3 cups cheese, and next 5 ingredients.
3. Spoon mixture into a lightly greased 1-qt. baking dish or lasagna pan. Top casserole with breadcrumbs.
4. Bake, uncovered, at 350° for 35 minutes. Sprinkle with remaining 1 cup cheese and almonds; bake 5 more minutes.

SHORTCUT SECRET

You can divide this casserole between 2 (11- x 7-inch) baking dishes. Bake as directed above, or freeze casseroles up to 1 month. Remove from freezer, and let stand at room temperature 1 hour. Bake, covered, at 350° for 30 minutes. Uncover casseroles, and bake 55 more minutes. Sprinkle with remaining 1 cup cheese and almonds, and bake 5 more minutes.

King Ranch Chicken Casserole

We've published several versions of this family favorite, and this one's the quickest yet. No sautéing is needed; just stir together the ingredients, and pop it in the oven.

MAKES 6 servings • **HANDS-ON TIME:** 13 min. • **TOTAL TIME:** 45 min.

- 2 cups chopped precooked chicken
- 1 (10¾-oz.) can cream of chicken soup
- 1 (10¾-oz.) can cream of mushroom soup
- 1 (10-oz.) package frozen seasoning blend
- 1 (10-oz.) can diced tomatoes and green chiles
- 1 tsp. chili powder
- ½ tsp. garlic salt
- 12 (6-inch) corn tortillas
- 2 cups (8 oz.) shredded Cheddar cheese

1. Preheat oven to 350°. Stir together first 7 ingredients.
2. Tear tortillas into 1-inch pieces; layer one-third of tortilla pieces in a lightly greased 13- x 9-inch baking dish. Top with one-third of chicken mixture and ⅔ cup cheese. Repeat layers twice.
3. Bake at 350° for 32 minutes or until casserole is thoroughly heated and bubbly.

Rediscovering the King Ranch Casserole brings back fond childhood memories.

Chicken-and-Corn Pies with Cornbread Crust

MAKES 5 servings • **HANDS-ON TIME:** 35 min. • **TOTAL TIME:** 1 hr., 5 min.

- 1 (10-oz.) can enchilada sauce
- 1 (10-oz.) can Mexican diced tomatoes with lime juice and cilantro, drained
- 2 cups frozen whole kernel corn
- 1 tsp. chili powder
- 3 cups chopped cooked chicken*
- 1 (6-oz.) package Mexican-style cornbread mix
- ⅔ cup milk
- 1 large egg
- 2 Tbsp. vegetable oil
- 1 cup (4 oz.) shredded Mexican four-cheese blend, divided

Toppings: sliced pickled jalapeño peppers, sour cream

1. Preheat oven to 375°. Stir together enchilada sauce and next 3 ingredients in a 3½-qt. saucepan over medium heat until combined; cook, stirring occasionally, 10 minutes. Stir in chicken.

2. Whisk together cornbread mix, next 3 ingredients, and ¾ cup cheese in a small bowl just until blended.

3. Pour chicken mixture into 5 lightly greased (10-oz.) ramekins. Spoon cornbread mixture over hot chicken mixture. Sprinkle evenly with remaining ¼ cup cheese. Place ramekins on jelly-roll pans.

4. Bake at 375° for 30 minutes or until golden and bubbly. Serve with desired toppings.

*2 (12.5-oz.) cans chicken, drained, may be substituted.

This pie may be prepared in a lightly greased 11- x 7-inch baking dish. Bake as directed, but without the jelly-roll pans.

Easy Enchiladas

Look for fresh salsa in the refrigerated section or the deli counter at your supermarket, or feel free to use your favorite jar of tomato salsa.

MAKES 4 servings • **HANDS-ON TIME:** 20 min. • **TOTAL TIME:** 50 min.

- 1 lb. ground turkey sausage*
- ½ cup chopped onion
- 1 tsp. minced garlic
- 1 (7-oz.) can tomatillo salsa, divided (we tested with La Costeña)
- ¼ cup chopped fresh cilantro
- 8 (6-inch) fajita-size corn tortillas**
- 2 cups (8 oz.) shredded Mexican four-cheese blend, divided
- Vegetable cooking spray
- 2 cups refrigerated fresh medium-heat tomato salsa
- ½ cup low-sodium chicken broth
- Garnish: chopped fresh cilantro

1. Preheat oven to 350°. Brown sausage in a large skillet over medium-high heat, stirring occasionally, 11 to 14 minutes or until meat crumbles and is no longer pink. Remove sausage from skillet using a slotted spoon, and drain on paper towels.
2. Sauté onion and garlic in hot drippings over medium-high heat 2 to 3 minutes or until onion is tender. Remove from heat. Stir in sausage, ½ cup tomatillo salsa, and ¼ cup chopped cilantro.
3. Place 2 tortillas between damp paper towels. Microwave tortillas at HIGH 15 seconds. Repeat procedure with remaining tortillas.
4. Spoon about ⅓ cup sausage mixture evenly down center of each softened tortilla, and sprinkle each with 1 Tbsp. cheese; roll tortillas up, and place, seam sides down, in a lightly greased 13- x 9-inch baking dish. Lightly coat tops of tortillas with cooking spray.
5. Bake at 350° for 20 to 25 minutes or until tortillas are crisp.
6. Stir together 2 cups tomato salsa, ½ cup chicken broth, and remaining tomatillo salsa in a medium saucepan over medium-high heat; cook, stirring occasionally, 4 to 6 minutes or until thoroughly heated. Pour salsa mixture over tortillas, and top evenly with remaining cheese. Bake 5 more minutes or until cheese is melted. Let stand 5 minutes. Garnish, if desired.
*Ground pork sausage may be substituted.
**8 (6-inch) fajita-size flour tortillas may be substituted, omitting Step 3.

Pizza Spaghetti Casserole

We prefer turkey pepperoni in this recipe. Freeze the unbaked casserole up to 1 month. Thaw overnight in the refrigerator; let stand 30 minutes at room temperature, and bake as directed.

make ahead

MAKES 6 servings • **HANDS-ON TIME:** 15 min. • **TOTAL TIME:** 55 min.

- 12 oz. uncooked spaghetti
- ½ tsp. salt
- 1 (1-lb.) package mild ground pork sausage
- 2 oz. turkey pepperoni slices (about 30), cut in half
- 1 (26-oz.) jar tomato-and-basil pasta sauce
- ¼ cup grated Parmesan cheese
- 1 (8-oz.) package shredded Italian three-cheese blend

1. Preheat oven to 350°. Cook spaghetti with ½ tsp. salt according to package directions. Drain well, and place in a lightly greased 13- x 9-inch baking dish.
2. Brown sausage in a large skillet over medium-high heat, stirring occasionally, 5 minutes or until sausage crumbles and is no longer pink. Drain and set aside. Wipe skillet clean. Add pepperoni, and cook over medium-high heat, stirring occasionally, 4 minutes or until slightly crisp.
3. Top spaghetti with sausage; pour pasta sauce over sausage. Arrange half of pepperoni slices evenly over pasta sauce. Sprinkle evenly with cheeses. Arrange remaining half of pepperoni slices evenly over cheese. Cover with nonstick or lightly greased aluminum foil.
4. Bake at 350° for 30 minutes; remove foil, and bake 10 more minutes or until cheese melts and just begins to brown.

The ultimate comfort food, this yummy dish tastes just like a pizza without the crust.

Tomato 'n' Beef Casserole with Polenta Crust

MAKES 6 servings • **HANDS-ON TIME:** 20 min. • **TOTAL TIME:** 1 hr., 25 min.

- 1 tsp. salt
- 1 cup plain yellow cornmeal
- ½ tsp. Montreal steak seasoning
- 1 cup (4 oz.) shredded sharp Cheddar cheese, divided
- 1 lb. ground chuck
- 1 cup chopped onion
- 1 medium zucchini, cut in half lengthwise and sliced (about 2 cups)
- 1 Tbsp. olive oil
- 2 (14½-oz.) cans petite diced tomatoes, drained
- 1 (6-oz.) can tomato paste
- 2 Tbsp. chopped fresh flat-leaf parsley

1. Preheat oven to 350°. Bring 3 cups water and 1 tsp. salt to a boil in a 2-qt. saucepan over medium-high heat. Whisk in cornmeal; reduce heat to low, and simmer, whisking constantly, 3 minutes or until thickened. Remove from heat, and stir in steak seasoning and ¼ cup Cheddar cheese. Spread cornmeal mixture into a lightly greased 11- x 7-inch baking dish.
2. Brown ground chuck in a large nonstick skillet over medium-high heat, stirring often, 10 minutes or until meat crumbles and is no longer pink; drain and transfer to a bowl.
3. Sauté onion and zucchini in hot oil in skillet over medium heat 5 minutes or until crisp-tender. Stir in beef, tomatoes, and tomato paste; simmer, stirring often, 10 minutes. Pour beef mixture over cornmeal crust. Sprinkle with remaining ¾ cup cheese.
4. Bake at 350° for 30 minutes or until bubbly. Sprinkle casserole with parsley just before serving.

Italian Casserole with Polenta Crust: Substitute Italian sausage for ground chuck and Italian six-cheese blend for Cheddar cheese. Prepare recipe as directed, sautéing 1 medium-size green bell pepper, chopped, with onion in Step 3.

Homestyle Ground Beef Casserole

Hamburger casserole works for any weeknight and is a universal family favorite.

make ahead

MAKES 6 servings • **HANDS-ON TIME:** 23 min. • **TOTAL TIME:** 1 hr., 18 min.

- 1 lb. ground round
- 1 (14½-oz.) can diced tomatoes with basil, garlic, and oregano, undrained
- 1 (10-oz.) can diced tomatoes and green chiles, undrained
- 1 (6-oz.) can tomato paste
- 1 tsp. salt
- ½ tsp. dried Italian seasoning
- ¼ tsp. pepper
- 3 cups uncooked medium egg noodles
- 5 green onions, chopped
- 1 (8-oz.) container sour cream
- 1 (3-oz.) package cream cheese, softened
- 1 cup (4 oz.) shredded sharp Cheddar cheese
- 1 cup (4 oz.) shredded Parmesan cheese
- 1 cup (4 oz.) shredded mozzarella cheese

1. Cook ground round in a large skillet over medium heat 8 minutes, stirring until meat crumbles and is no longer pink. Stir in both cans diced tomatoes and next 4 ingredients. Bring to a boil; reduce heat, and simmer, uncovered, 5 minutes. Remove from heat; set aside.
2. Preheat oven to 350°. Prepare egg noodles in boiling salted water according to package directions. Stir together hot cooked noodles, chopped green onions, sour cream, and cream cheese until blended.
3. Spoon egg noodles into a lightly greased 13- x 9-inch or other similar-size baking dish. Top with beef mixture; sprinkle with shredded cheeses in order listed.
4. Bake, uncovered, at 350° for 35 minutes. Uncover and bake 5 more minutes. Let stand 10 to 15 minutes before serving.

SHORTCUT SECRET

Freeze assembled, unbaked casserole up to 1 month, if desired. Thaw in refrigerator overnight. Bake as directed.

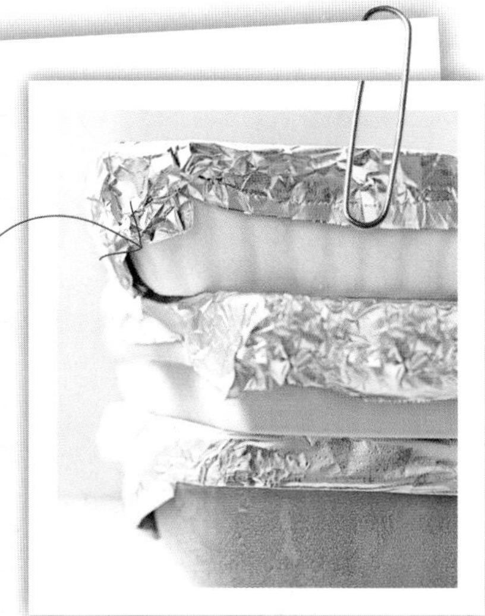

Tex-Mex Lasagna

MAKES 8 servings • **HANDS-ON TIME:** 30 min. • **TOTAL TIME:** 1 hr., 15 min.

- 1 lb. lean ground beef
- 1 cup frozen diced onion, red and green bell pepper, and celery
- 3 garlic cloves, minced
- 1 Tbsp. chili powder
- 1 tsp. salt-free chipotle seasoning blend
- 1 (24-oz.) jar mild salsa
- 1 (15-oz.) can dark red kidney beans, drained
- 1 (10-oz.) can enchilada sauce
- 1 (10-oz.) package frozen whole kernel corn, thawed
- 16 (6-inch) fajita-size corn tortillas
- 4 cups (16 oz.) shredded Mexican four-cheese blend

Garnish: cilantro

Toppings: sour cream, chopped tomatoes

1. Preheat oven to 350°. Cook first 5 ingredients in a large nonstick skillet over medium-high heat, stirring often, 10 to 12 minutes or until vegetables are tender and meat crumbles and is no longer pink.

2. Stir in salsa and next 3 ingredients. Cook 5 to 10 minutes or until thoroughly heated.

3. Layer 1 cup beef mixture, 2 tortillas (overlapping edges), and ½ cup cheese in a lightly greased 7- x 5- x 1½-inch baking dish. Repeat layers once. Repeat procedure with 3 additional 7- x 5- x 1½-inch baking dishes. Cover dishes with nonstick aluminum foil.

4. Bake, covered, at 350° for 30 minutes; uncover and bake 5 more minutes or until bubbly. Let stand 10 minutes before serving. Garnish, if desired. Serve with desired toppings.

SHORTCUT SECRET

To use a lightly greased 13- x 9-inch baking dish, prepare recipe through Step 2. Omit 4 corn tortillas. Layer one-third of beef mixture, 6 tortillas (overlapping edges), and 2 cups cheese. Repeat layers with one-third of beef mixture, remaining 6 tortillas, remaining beef mixture, and remaining 2 cups cheese. Bake, covered, at 350° for 40 minutes; uncover and bake 10 more minutes or until bubbly. Let stand 10 minutes before serving.

Scalloped Potatoes with Ham

MAKES 6 servings • **HANDS-ON TIME:** 20 min. • **TOTAL TIME:** 1 hr., 40 min.

- 1 medium onion, chopped
- 1 Tbsp. vegetable oil
- 3 garlic cloves, finely chopped
- 2 sweet potatoes, peeled and cut into ¼-inch slices (about 1½ lb.)
- 2 baking potatoes, peeled and cut into ¼-inch slices (about 1½ lb.)
- ½ cup all-purpose flour
- 1 tsp. salt
- ¼ tsp. pepper
- 2 cups chopped cooked ham
- 2 cups (8 oz.) shredded Gruyère cheese, divided
- 1¾ cups whipping cream
- 2 Tbsp. butter, cut into pieces

1. Preheat oven to 400°. Sauté onion in oil over medium-high heat 5 minutes or until tender. Add garlic; cook 30 seconds. Remove from heat, and set aside. Place potatoes in a large bowl.
2. Combine flour, salt, and pepper; sprinkle over potatoes, tossing to coat. Arrange half of potato mixture in a greased 13- x 9-inch baking dish or 3-qt. gratin dish. Top with onion, ham, and 1 cup cheese. Top with remaining potato mixture. Pour cream over potato mixture. Dot with butter, and cover with aluminum foil.
3. Bake at 400° for 50 minutes. Uncover, top with remaining 1 cup cheese, and bake 20 more minutes or until potatoes are tender and cheese is browned. Let stand 10 minutes before serving.

Nutty Gruyère cheese and sweet potatoes give this dish fresh appeal.

Shrimp Casserole

MAKES 8 servings • **HANDS-ON TIME:** 30 min. • **TOTAL TIME:** 1 hr., 12 min.

- **1½ cups uncooked long-grain rice**
- **1½ lb. medium-size raw shrimp**
- **½ cup butter**
- **1 green bell pepper, chopped**
- **1 onion, chopped**
- **3 celery ribs, chopped**
- **2 garlic cloves, minced**
- **4 green onions, chopped**
- **2 (10¾-oz.) cans cream of shrimp soup, undiluted***
- **¼ tsp. salt**
- **¼ tsp. freshly ground black pepper**
- **1 cup (4 oz.) shredded Cheddar-colby cheese blend**
- **¼ cup fine, dry breadcrumbs**

1. Preheat oven to 350°. Prepare rice according to package directions.
2. Peel shrimp, and devein, if desired.
3. Melt butter in a large skillet over medium heat; add bell pepper and next 4 ingredients, and sauté 10 to 12 minutes or until tender. Stir in soup, shrimp, salt, and black pepper; cook 3 minutes or just until shrimp turn pink. (Do not overcook.)
4. Combine shrimp mixture and rice. Pour mixture into a lightly greased 13- x 9-inch baking dish. Sprinkle evenly with 1 cup shredded cheese and ¼ cup breadcrumbs.
5. Bake at 350° for 25 minutes or until cheese is melted.
*2 (10¾-oz.) cans cream of celery soup, undiluted, may be substituted.

Chicken Casserole: Substitute 3 cups chopped cooked chicken for shrimp and 2 (10¾-oz.) cans cream of chicken soup, undiluted, for cream of shrimp soup. Proceed with recipe as directed.

How To Chop an Onion

Trim the stem and root ends; discard. Remove the papery outer skins. Stand the onion upright on a cutting board and cut a thin slice off 1 side. Make vertical slices through the onion to within ¼ inch of the bottom. Rotate the onion 90 degrees and repeat. Finally, turn the onion so that the cut side is flat on the board. Cut vertically through the onion.

Cajun Shrimp Casserole

This longer ingredient list is worth the effort for a special occasion meal. If you're not a fan of okra, you can leave it out of this dish.

make ahead

MAKES 6 servings • **HANDS-ON TIME:** 30 min. • **TOTAL TIME:** 1 hr., 6 min.

- 2 lb. unpeeled, large fresh shrimp
- ¼ cup butter
- 1 small red onion, chopped*
- ½ cup chopped red bell pepper*
- ½ cup chopped yellow bell pepper*
- ½ cup chopped green bell pepper*
- 4 garlic cloves, minced
- 2 cups fresh or frozen sliced okra
- 1 Tbsp. lemon juice
- 1½ tsp. salt
- 3 cups cooked long-grain rice
- 1 (10¾-oz.) can cream of shrimp soup**
- ½ cup dry white wine
- 1 Tbsp. soy sauce
- ½ tsp. cayenne pepper
- ¼ cup grated Parmesan cheese
- Garnishes: quartered lemon slices, chopped parsley leaves

1. Preheat oven to 350°. Peel shrimp; devein, if desired.

2. Melt ¼ cup butter in a large skillet over medium-high heat. Add onion and next 3 ingredients; sauté 7 minutes or until tender. Add garlic, and sauté 1 minute. Stir in okra, lemon juice, and salt; sauté 5 minutes. Add shrimp, and cook 3 minutes or until shrimp turn pink. Stir in rice and next 4 ingredients until blended. Pour into a lightly greased 11- x 7-inch baking dish. Sprinkle evenly with Parmesan cheese.

3. Bake at 350° for 15 to 20 minutes or until casserole is bubbly and cheese is lightly browned. Garnish, if desired.

*1 (10-oz.) package frozen onions and peppers may be substituted for fresh onion and bell peppers.

**1 (10¾-oz.) can cream of mushroom soup may be substituted for cream of shrimp soup.

SHORTCUT SECRET

An unbaked casserole may be made 1 day in advance. Cover and refrigerate. Let stand at room temperature 30 minutes before baking as directed. To freeze an unbaked casserole, prepare as directed, omitting Parmesan cheese. Cover tightly, and freeze. Let stand at room temperature 30 minutes before baking. Bake, covered, at 350° for 50 minutes. Uncover; sprinkle evenly with Parmesan cheese, and bake 10 more minutes or until cheese is lightly browned.

One-Pot Pasta

MAKES 4 servings • **HANDS-ON TIME:** 10 min. • **TOTAL TIME:** 38 min.

- 1 lb. lean ground beef
- 1 small onion, diced
- 1 (8-oz.) package sliced fresh mushrooms
- 1 tsp. vegetable oil
- 2 garlic cloves, minced
- 2 (26-oz.) jars tomato-and-basil pasta sauce (we tested with Classico)
- 1 Tbsp. dried Italian seasoning
- ½ tsp. salt
- ¼ tsp. pepper
- 1 (20-oz.) package refrigerated four-cheese ravioli (we tested with Buitoni)
- 1 cup (4 oz.) shredded mozzarella cheese

1. Cook ground beef in a Dutch oven over medium-high heat, stirring until meat crumbles and is no longer pink; drain. Wipe Dutch oven clean.
2. Sauté onion and mushrooms in hot oil over medium-high heat 8 minutes or until tender. Add garlic, and sauté 1 minute. Stir in beef, pasta sauce, next 3 ingredients, and 1 cup water.
3. Bring sauce to a boil; add ravioli. Reduce heat to medium-low; cover, and simmer, stirring occasionally, 8 to 10 minutes or until pasta is done. Stir in cheese. Serve immediately.

To prevent filled pastas such as ravioli from breaking open when cooking, add to gently boiling water, and simmer.

Italian Jambalaya

MAKES 6 to 8 servings • **HANDS-ON TIME:** 20 min. • **TOTAL TIME:** 55 min.

- 1 lb. Italian sausage, casings removed
- 2 skinned and boned chicken breasts, coarsely chopped (about 1 lb.)
- 2 boneless center-cut pork chops, chopped (about 1 lb.)
- 1 (10-oz.) package frozen diced onion, red and green bell peppers, and celery
- 3 garlic cloves, minced
- 1 Tbsp. dried Italian seasoning
- 1 tsp. salt
- ½ tsp. black pepper
- 2 (10-oz.) cans diced tomatoes and green chiles
- 1 (6-oz.) can tomato paste
- Hot cooked orzo or other pasta (about 8 oz. uncooked)
- Garnishes: thinly sliced green onions, shredded Parmesan cheese

1. Brown Italian sausage in a Dutch oven over medium-high heat, stirring often, 5 minutes or until sausage crumbles and is no longer pink. Remove sausage from Dutch oven using a slotted spoon, reserving drippings in Dutch oven.
2. Cook chicken and pork in hot drippings in Dutch oven over medium-high heat, stirring often, 4 to 5 minutes or until browned on all sides. Add frozen onion mixture and next 4 ingredients, and sauté 5 minutes. Stir in diced tomatoes and green chiles, tomato paste, ¼ cup water, and Italian sausage; cover, reduce heat to low, and cook, stirring often, 20 minutes.
3. Stir hot cooked orzo into jambalaya just before serving, or serve over hot cooked pasta. Garnish, if desired.

Orzo pasta replaces rice in this twist on a Creole favorite. The sauce is also delicious over hot cooked spaghetti.

cooker

SUPPERS

Open-Faced Meatball Sandwiches

These sandwiches are so versatile that they even please the pickiest eater at the dinner table. Just add your favorite pasta sauce and cheese to the meatball mixture, and serve over sesame, sourdough, white, or whole-wheat hoagies.

MAKES 6 servings • **HANDS-ON TIME:** 5 min. • **TOTAL TIME:** 6 hr., 5 min.

- 24 frozen cooked Italian-style meatballs, thawed (we tested with Mama Mia)
- 1 (26-oz.) jar super chunky mushroom pasta sauce (we tested with Ragú Chunky Garden)
- 1 (15-oz.) can Italian-style tomato sauce (we tested with Hunt's Family Favorites)
- 1 (5.5-oz.) can spicy tomato juice (we tested with V8)
- 6 (6-inch) hoagie rolls, split but not cut through, and toasted
- 1½ cups (6 oz.) shredded mozzarella cheese

1. Combine first 4 ingredients in a 3-qt. slow cooker.
2. Cover and cook on HIGH 1 hour. Reduce heat to LOW, and cook 4½ to 5 hours or until slightly thickened. Spoon meatball mixture evenly into rolls. Sprinkle with cheese.

Slow-Cooker Sloppy Joes

MAKES 8 servings • **HANDS-ON TIME:** 14 min. • **TOTAL TIME:** 4 hr., 14 min.

- 1½ lb. lean ground beef
- 1 (16-oz.) package ground pork sausage
- 1 small onion, chopped
- ½ medium-size green bell pepper, chopped
- 1 (8-oz.) can tomato sauce
- ½ cup ketchup
- ¼ cup firmly packed brown sugar
- ¼ cup all-purpose flour
- 2 Tbsp. cider vinegar
- 2 Tbsp. yellow mustard
- 1 Tbsp. chili powder
- 1 Tbsp. Worcestershire sauce
- ½ tsp. salt
- 8 hamburger buns, toasted

1. Brown beef and sausage with onion and bell pepper in a large Dutch oven over medium-high heat, stirring 10 minutes or until beef and sausage crumble and are no longer pink. Drain well.
2. Place beef mixture in a 4-qt. slow cooker. Stir in ½ cup water, tomato sauce, and next 8 ingredients. Cover and cook on HIGH 4 hours. Serve on hamburger buns.

Slow-Cooker Sloppy Joes

Swiss Steak

MAKES 4 servings • **HANDS-ON TIME:** 15 min. • **TOTAL TIME:** 8 hr., 15 min.

- 5 bacon slices, halved
- 2 (8-oz.) containers refrigerated prechopped celery, onion, and bell pepper mix
- 2 Tbsp. jarred minced garlic
- 1¼ lb. bottom round steak (about 1 inch thick), cut into 4 equal portions
- ⅓ cup all-purpose flour
- 1½ tsp. salt
- ¾ tsp. freshly ground pepper
- 1 (14-oz.) can beef broth
- 1 (14.5-oz.) can diced fire-roasted tomatoes, undrained
- 1 Tbsp. Worcestershire sauce
- 1 tsp. dried Italian seasoning

1. Cook bacon in a large nonstick skillet over medium-high heat 5 to 6 minutes or until crisp; remove bacon, and drain on paper towels, reserving drippings in skillet. Crumble bacon; set aside. Cook celery mix and garlic in hot drippings, stirring often, until tender. Transfer vegetables to a 5-qt. slow cooker, using a slotted spoon. Reserve drippings in pan.
2. While vegetables cook, place meat on a sheet of plastic wrap, and flatten to ¼-inch thickness, using the pointed side of a meat mallet. Combine flour, salt, and pepper in a shallow dish. Dredge meat in flour mixture; cook in hot drippings 3 minutes on each side or until browned.
3. Place meat in slow cooker over vegetables, reserving drippings in skillet. Add beef broth and next 3 ingredients to skillet, stirring to loosen particles from bottom of skillet. Pour broth mixture over beef in slow cooker. Cover and cook on LOW 8 hours or until beef is very tender. Sprinkle with crumbled bacon before serving.

Serve this comforting supper over mashed potatoes and spoon with extra sauce.

Slow-Cooker Beef Tacos

We brown the beef before slow cooking to add color and enhance flavor.

kids' favorite

MAKES 8 servings • **HANDS-ON TIME:** 20 min. • **TOTAL TIME:** 6 hr., 30 min.

- 2 lb. boneless beef chuck roast, cut into 1-inch cubes
- 1 tsp. salt
- 1 Tbsp. vegetable oil
- 1 Tbsp. chili powder
- 1 (6-oz.) can tomato paste
- 2 cups beef broth
- 1 small white onion, chopped
- 1 (8-oz.) can tomato sauce
- ½ medium-size green bell pepper, chopped
- 1 tsp. ground cumin
- ½ tsp. pepper
- Flour or corn tortillas, warmed
- Toppings: shredded Cheddar or Monterey Jack cheese, sour cream, chopped cilantro

1. Sprinkle beef evenly with salt.
2. Cook beef, in batches, in hot oil in a Dutch oven over medium-high heat 5 to 7 minutes or until browned on all sides. Remove beef, reserving drippings in Dutch oven. Add 1 Tbsp. chili powder to Dutch oven; cook, stirring constantly, 1 minute. Stir in tomato paste, and cook, stirring constantly, 2 minutes. Add 2 cups beef broth, stirring to loosen particles from bottom of Dutch oven. Return beef to Dutch oven, and stir.
3. Place beef mixture in a 4½-qt. slow cooker. Add onion and next 4 ingredients. Cook on HIGH 4 hours or on LOW 6 hours or until beef is tender. Serve with warm tortillas and desired toppings.

This mixture is also great over baked potatoes with your favorite toppings.

Steak Soup

MAKES 6 servings • **HANDS-ON TIME:** 15 min. • **TOTAL TIME:** 8 hr., 15 min.

- 2¼ lb. sirloin tip roast, cut into 1-inch cubes
- ¼ cup all-purpose flour
- ½ tsp. salt
- ½ tsp. coarsely ground pepper
- 2 Tbsp. canola oil
- 1 (1-oz.) envelope dry onion soup mix
- 4 cups beef broth
- 1 Tbsp. tomato paste
- 1 Tbsp. Worcestershire sauce
- 2 cups uncooked wide egg noodles

1. Combine first 4 ingredients in a large zip-top plastic freezer bag; seal bag, and shake to coat beef.
2. Saute beef in hot oil in a dutch oven over medium-high heat 6 minutes or until browned. Place in a 4-qt. slow cooker. Sprinkle onion soup mix over beef. Whisk together beef broth, tomato paste, and Worcestershire sauce; pour over beef. Cover and cook on LOW 8 hours or until beef is tender.
3. Add noodles to slow cooker; cover and cook 30 minutes or until noodles are done.

Sirloin tip is a leaner cut than traditional chuck roast. It yields a very tender "fall-apart" texture after the long, slow cooking.

Slow-Cooker Barbecue Beef Sandwiches

Freeze any leftover meat for up to 1 month.

MAKES 12 servings • **HANDS-ON TIME:** 15 min. • **TOTAL TIME:** 7 hr., 15 min.

- **1 (3½-lb.) eye-of-round roast, cut in half vertically**
- **2 tsp. salt, divided**
- **2 garlic cloves, pressed**
- **1 (10-oz.) can condensed beef broth**
- **1 cup ketchup**
- **½ cup firmly packed brown sugar**
- **½ cup lemon juice**
- **3 Tbsp. steak sauce**
- **1 tsp. coarsely ground pepper**
- **1 tsp. Worcestershire sauce**
- **12 kaiser rolls or sandwich buns**
- **Dill pickle slices**

1. Sprinkle beef evenly with 1 tsp. salt.
2. Stir together remaining 1 tsp. salt, garlic, and next 7 ingredients. Pour half of mixture into a 5½-qt. slow cooker. Place beef in slow cooker, and pour remaining mixture over beef.
3. Cover and cook on HIGH 7 hours.
4. Shred beef in slow cooker with 2 forks. Serve in rolls or buns with dill pickle slices.

How To Press Fresh Garlic

Use a garlic press to prep fresh garlic. Just place a peeled clove in the gadget, and press to force through the tiny holes.

Beef with Red Wine Sauce

Beef with Red Wine Sauce

MAKES 6 servings • **HANDS-ON TIME:** 15 min. • **TOTAL TIME:** 6 hr., 15 min.

- 3 lb. boneless beef chuck roast, cut into 1-inch pieces
- 1 medium onion, sliced
- 1 lb. fresh mushrooms, halved
- 1 (1.61-oz.) package brown gravy mix
- 1 (10½-oz.) can beef broth
- 1 cup red wine
- 2 Tbsp. tomato paste
- 1 bay leaf
- Hot cooked egg noodles or rice
- Garnish: chopped fresh parsley

1. Place first 3 ingredients in a 6-qt. slow cooker.
2. Whisk together gravy mix and next 3 ingredients; pour evenly over beef and vegetables. Add bay leaf.
3. Cover and cook on HIGH 6 hours. Remove and discard bay leaf. Serve over noodles or rice. Garnish, if desired.

Beef with Olives

MAKES 8 to 10 servings • **HANDS-ON TIME:** 15 min. • **TOTAL TIME:** 5 hr., 15 min.

- ¼ cup butter, melted
- 3 lb. boneless top sirloin steak, cut into 1½-inch pieces
- ½ tsp. pepper
- ¼ tsp. salt
- 1 Tbsp. olive oil
- 3 large garlic cloves, sliced
- 2 shallots, vertically sliced
- 2 cups pimiento-stuffed Spanish olives
- 2 Tbsp. olive juice from jar
- 1 (12-oz.) jar roasted red bell peppers, drained and cut into thick strips
- Hot cooked rice

1. Pour melted butter into a 4- or 5-qt. slow cooker.
2. Sprinkle beef with pepper and salt. Heat oil in a large skillet over medium-high heat. Cook beef, in 2 batches, 2 minutes on each side. Place beef in slow cooker. Add garlic and shallots to skillet; sauté 1 minute over medium-high heat. Spoon over beef in slow cooker. Coarsely chop 1 cup olives. Sprinkle chopped and whole olives and olive juice over beef.
3. Cover and cook on LOW 5 hours or until beef is tender. Stir in roasted bell peppers just before serving. Serve over hot cooked rice.

Cowboy Pot Roast

MAKES 6 servings • **HANDS-ON TIME:** 15 min. • **TOTAL TIME:** 8 hr., 45 min.

- 1½ tsp. salt, divided
- 1½ tsp. pepper, divided
- 1 (14.5-oz.) can petite-cut diced tomatoes, drained
- 1 (10-oz.) can diced tomatoes and green chiles, undrained
- 1 onion, cut into 8 wedges
- 1 Tbsp. chili powder
- 1 (2½- to 3-lb.) eye-of-round roast, trimmed
- 2 Tbsp. vegetable oil
- 2 (16-oz.) cans pinto beans, drained
- 1 (15-oz.) can black beans, drained
- Pickled jalapeño pepper slices (optional)

1. Combine 1 tsp. salt, 1 tsp. pepper, and next 4 ingredients in a medium bowl. Sprinkle roast with remaining ½ tsp. salt and ½ tsp. pepper. Brown roast on all sides in hot oil in a large Dutch oven over medium-high heat. Transfer roast to a 5- or 6-qt. slow cooker. Pour tomato mixture over roast. Cover and cook on LOW 8 to 10 hours or until very tender.

2. Remove roast from slow cooker, and cut into large chunks; keep warm.

3. Skim fat from juices in slow cooker. Mash 1½ cans (about 2¾ cups) pinto beans; add to slow cooker, and stir until combined. Stir in black beans and remaining ½ can pinto beans. Add roast pieces back to slow cooker; cover and cook on HIGH 20 more minutes. Top each serving with jalapeño pepper slices, if desired.

Browning the meat before slow cooking enhances both the appearance and flavor of the meat.

12 FL. OZ.

Italian Pot Roast

Italian Pot Roast

company's coming

MAKES 6 servings • **HANDS-ON TIME:** 18 min. • **TOTAL TIME:** 8 hr., 58 min.

- 1 (8-oz.) package sliced fresh mushrooms
- 1 large sweet onion, cut in half and sliced
- 1 (3- to 4-lb.) boneless chuck roast, trimmed
- 1 tsp. pepper
- 2 Tbsp. olive oil
- 1 (1-oz.) envelope dry onion soup mix
- 1 (14-oz.) can beef broth
- 1 (8-oz.) can tomato sauce
- 3 Tbsp. tomato paste
- 1 tsp. dried Italian seasoning
- 2 Tbsp. cornstarch

1. Place mushrooms and onion in a lightly greased 5- to 6-qt. slow cooker. Sprinkle roast with pepper. Cook roast in hot oil in a large skillet over medium-high heat 2 to 3 minutes on each side or until browned.
2. Place roast on top of mushrooms and onion in slow cooker. Sprinkle onion soup mix over roast; pour beef broth and tomato sauce over roast. Cover and cook on LOW 8 to 10 hours or until meat shreds easily with a fork.
3. Transfer roast to a cutting board; cut into large chunks, removing any large pieces of fat. Keep roast warm.
4. Skim fat from juices in slow cooker; stir in tomato paste and Italian seasoning. Stir together cornstarch and 2 Tbsp. water in a small bowl until smooth; add to juices in slow cooker, stirring until blended. Increase heat to HIGH. Cover and cook 40 minutes or until mixture is thickened. Stir in roast.

Pork Carnita Nachos

MAKES 4 servings • **HANDS-ON TIME:** 10 min. • **TOTAL TIME:** 6 hr., 10 min.

- 1 onion, sliced
- 2 Tbsp. chopped canned chipotle peppers in adobo sauce or 2 fresh jalapeño peppers, seeded and sliced
- 2 to 3 lb. boned pork butt or shoulder
- 4 garlic cloves, slivered
- Salt and pepper to taste
- 1 Tbsp. vegetable oil
- Tortilla chips
- Toppings: jalapeños, shredded Monterey Jack cheese, salsa verde, fresh salsa

1. Combine onion, chipotle peppers or jalapenos, and ¼ cup water in a 5-qt. slow cooker. Using a knife, make slits all over pork and insert garlic. Season roast with salt and pepper. Heat a large Dutch oven over medium-high heat; add oil. Brown roast on all sides, about 8 minutes. Transfer roast to slow cooker. Pour ½ cup water into pan, stirring over low heat, using a wooden spoon, to loosen browned particles from bottom of Dutch oven. Pour liquid into slow cooker. Cover and cook on HIGH for 6 hours.
2. Remove roast from slow cooker; let cool. Shred pork, using two forks. Return pulled pork to slow cooker, stirring to combine. Serve pork over tortilla chips and with desired toppings.

Chalupa Dinner Bowl

This pork-and-bean mixture is versatile. Serve it spooned over cornbread or rolled up burrito-style in flour tortillas. Make hearty nachos, quesadillas, or tacos with it, too. It can even be used as a meaty addition to huevos rancheros (fried corn tortillas topped with fried eggs and salsa).

MAKES 8 servings • **HANDS-ON TIME:** 30 min. • **TOTAL TIME:** 11 hr., 35 min.

- 1 lb. dried pinto beans
- 1 (3½-lb.) bone-in pork loin roast
- 2 (4-oz.) cans chopped green chiles
- 2 garlic cloves, chopped
- 1 Tbsp. chili powder
- 2 tsp. salt
- 1 tsp. dried oregano
- 1 tsp. ground cumin
- 1 (32-oz.) box chicken broth
- 1 (10-oz.) can diced tomatoes and green chiles with lime juice and cilantro (we tested with Rotel)
- 8 taco salad shells
- 1 small head iceberg lettuce, shredded
- Toppings: shredded Monterey Jack cheese, pickled jalapeño pepper slices, halved grape tomatoes, sour cream, sliced avocado

1. Rinse and sort beans according to package directions.
2. Place pinto beans in a 6-qt. slow cooker; add roast and next 6 ingredients. Pour chicken broth evenly over top of roast.
3. Cover and cook on HIGH 1 hour; reduce heat to LOW, and cook 9 hours. Or, cover and cook on HIGH 6 hours. Remove bones and fat from roast; pull roast into large pieces with 2 forks. Stir in diced tomatoes and green chiles. Cook, uncovered, on HIGH 1 more hour or until liquid is slightly thickened.
4. Heat taco salad shells according to package directions; place shredded lettuce evenly into shells. Spoon about 1 cup pork-and-bean mixture into each shell using a slotted spoon. Serve with desired toppings.

Thai-Style Ribs

Thai-Style Ribs

MAKES 2 to 4 servings • **HANDS-ON TIME:** 10 min. • **TOTAL TIME:** 14 hr., 10 min.

- 3½ lb. pork baby back ribs, racks cut in half
- 1 (11.5-oz.) can frozen orange-pineapple-apple juice concentrate, thawed and undiluted (we tested with Welch's)
- ¾ cup soy sauce
- ¼ cup creamy peanut butter
- ¼ cup minced fresh cilantro
- 2 Tbsp. minced fresh ginger
- 2 tsp. sugar
- 1 garlic clove, pressed
- Garnish: fresh cilantro sprigs

1. Place ribs in a large shallow dish or zip-top freezer bag.
2. Whisk together juice concentrate and next 6 ingredients in a small bowl. Reserve ¾ cup mixture in refrigerator for dipping. Pour remaining mixture evenly over ribs; cover or seal, and chill 8 hours, turning occasionally.
3. Remove ribs from marinade, discarding marinade. Place 1 rack of ribs in bottom of a 6-qt. slow cooker; stand remaining ribs on their sides around edges of slow cooker. Cover and cook on HIGH 1 hour. Reduce heat to LOW, and cook 5 hours.
4. Microwave reserved ¾ cup sauce in a 1-cup glass measure at HIGH 1 to 1½ minutes or until thoroughly heated, stirring once. Serve with ribs. Garnish, if desired.

Classic Barbecue Ribs

Turn the slow cooker on before you leave for work, or cook the ribs overnight and refrigerate until dinnertime. If you make this recipe a day ahead, refrigerate overnight and remove fat from the sauce before reheating. If you reheat in the microwave, use 50% power.

MAKES 4 to 6 servings • **HANDS-ON TIME:** 15 min. • **TOTAL TIME:** 6 hr., 15 min.

- 4 lb. bone-in country-style pork ribs
- 2 tsp. salt, divided
- 1 medium onion, chopped
- 1 cup firmly packed light brown sugar
- 1 cup apple butter
- 1 cup ketchup
- ½ cup lemon juice
- ½ cup orange juice
- 1 Tbsp. steak sauce (we tested with A.1.)
- 1 tsp. coarsely ground pepper
- 1 tsp. minced garlic
- ½ tsp. Worcestershire sauce
- Garnish: chopped fresh parsley

1. Cut ribs apart, if necessary, and trim excess fat; sprinkle 1 tsp. salt evenly over ribs.
2. Stir together remaining 1 tsp. salt, onion, and next 9 ingredients until blended. Pour half of onion mixture into a 5-qt. slow cooker. Place ribs in slow cooker, and pour remaining mixture over ribs.
3. Cover and cook on HIGH 6 to 7 hours or until ribs are tender. Garnish, if desired.

Slow-Cooked Cajun Dirty Rice

MAKES 8 servings • **HANDS-ON TIME:** 10 min. • **TOTAL TIME:** 2 hr., 10 min.

- 1 lb. lean ground beef
- 1 lb. ground pork sausage
- 2 tsp. Cajun seasoning
- 2 (8-oz.) containers refrigerated prechopped celery, onion, and bell pepper mix
- 2 cups uncooked long-grain rice
- 1 (10-oz.) can diced tomatoes with green chiles, undrained
- 1 cup chicken broth
- ¼ tsp. ground red pepper

1. Brown first 3 ingredients in a large skillet over medium-high heat, stirring often, 8 minutes or until meat crumbles and is no longer pink. Transfer meat mixture to a 5-qt. slow cooker, using a slotted spoon.

2. Stir in celery mix and remaining ingredients. Cover and cook on LOW 2 hours or until liquid is absorbed and rice is tender.

SHORTCUT SECRET

Cooking the rice in the slow cooker along with the rest of the ingredients is a big timesaver compared to cooking it separately on the side. A common mistake in cooking rice from scratch is to add too much liquid, which can make it gummy. There's not a lot of liquid in this recipe to start with, but the tomatoes and vegetables produce just enough to steam the rice.

Slow-Cooker King Ranch Chicken

MAKES 6 servings • **HANDS-ON TIME:** 10 min. • **TOTAL TIME:** 4 hr., 10 min.

- 4 cups chopped cooked chicken
- 1 large onion, chopped
- 1 large green bell pepper, chopped
- 1 (10$\frac{3}{4}$-oz.) can cream of chicken soup
- 1 (10$\frac{3}{4}$-oz.) can cream of mushroom soup
- 1 (10-oz.) can diced tomatoes and green chiles
- 1 tsp. chili powder
- 1 garlic clove, minced
- 12 (6-inch) fajita-size corn tortillas
- 2 cups (8 oz.) shredded sharp Cheddar cheese

1. Stir together first 8 ingredients. Tear tortillas into 1-inch pieces; layer one-third of tortilla pieces in a lightly greased 6-qt. slow cooker. Top with one-third of chicken mixture and $\frac{2}{3}$ cup cheese. Repeat layers twice.

2. Cover and cook on LOW 3$\frac{1}{2}$ hours or until bubbly and edges are golden brown. Uncover and cook on LOW 30 minutes.

Removing the slow cooker's lid during the last 30 minutes of cooking gives this casserole oven-baked flavor and texture.

Chicken and Cranberry Dressing

MAKES 8 to 10 servings • **HANDS-ON TIME:** 15 min. • **TOTAL TIME:** 7 hr., 15 min.

- 1 slow-cooker liner
- Vegetable cooking spray
- 6 cups crumbled cornbread
- 4 cups chopped or shredded cooked chicken
- 2 cups frozen chopped celery, onion, and bell pepper mix
- 1½ cups dried cranberries or cherries
- 8 slices firm white bread, torn into bite-size pieces
- 3 large eggs, lightly beaten
- 2 (14-oz.) cans chicken broth
- 2 (10¾-oz.) cans cream of chicken soup
- ½ tsp. freshly ground pepper
- ⅓ cup butter, cut into pieces
- Garnish: whole-berry cranberry sauce

1. Place a slow-cooker liner in a 5- or 6-qt. slow cooker. Coat liner with cooking spray. Place cornbread in liner. Add chicken and next 7 ingredients; toss gently. Dot with butter.

2. Cover and cook on HIGH 4 hours or on LOW 7 hours or until dressing is puffed and set in center. Rotate slow cooker insert halfway after 2 hours. Stir before serving. Garnish, if desired.

Chicken Enchilada Dip

The corn tortillas cook into this dish and thicken it—you won't see them after they're cooked, but you will still taste their authentic Mexican flavor.

MAKES 8 servings • **HANDS-ON TIME:** 10 min. • **TOTAL TIME:** 4 hr., 10 min.

- 2 (10-oz.) cans mild green chile enchilada sauce
- 10 (6-inch) corn tortillas, torn into 3-inch pieces
- 4 cups pulled cooked chicken breasts
- 1½ cups sour cream
- 1 (12-oz.) package shredded colby-Jack cheese blend, divided
- 1 (10¾-oz.) can cream of mushroom soup
- 8 cups shredded iceberg lettuce
- 1 (15-oz.) can black beans
- 3 tomatoes, diced

1. Spoon ½ cup enchilada sauce over bottom of a greased 4-qt. slow cooker. Add enough tortilla pieces to cover sauce.
2. Stir together chicken, sour cream, 2 cups cheese, and soup. Spread 2 cups chicken mixture over tortilla pieces. Top with tortilla pieces to cover. Drizzle with ½ cup enchilada sauce. Repeat layers twice, ending with tortilla pieces and remaining enchilada sauce.
Sprinkle with remaining 1 cup cheese.
3. Cover and cook on LOW 4 hours. Place lettuce on plates; top with chicken, beans, and tomatoes. Serve hot.

SHOPPER'S COMPANION

When buying tomatoes, don't let looks fool you—some of the best-tasting tomatoes are not the prettiest. To find the tastiest tomatoes, smell them; a good tomato should smell like a tomato, especially at the stem end.

Braised Chicken Thighs with Carrots and Potatoes

MAKES 6 servings • **HANDS-ON TIME:** 20 min. • **TOTAL TIME:** 7 hr., 20 min.

- 1 medium onion, halved lengthwise and sliced
- 4 medium-size new potatoes (about 1 lb.), cut into ¼-inch-thick slices
- 2 cups baby carrots
- 1¼ tsp. salt, divided
- ½ tsp. pepper, divided
- ¼ cup chicken broth
- ¼ cup white wine
- 1 tsp. minced garlic
- ½ tsp. dried thyme
- 1 tsp. paprika
- 6 skinned, bone-in chicken thighs (about 1½ to 1¾ lb.)
- Garnish: lemon slices

1. Place onion in a lightly greased 6-qt. slow cooker; top with potatoes and carrots. Combine ¾ tsp. salt, ¼ tsp. pepper, broth, and next 3 ingredients. Pour broth mixture over vegetables. Combine paprika, remaining ½ tsp. salt, and remaining ¼ tsp. pepper; rub evenly over chicken thighs, and arrange on top of vegetables.
2. Cover and cook on HIGH 1 hour; reduce heat to LOW, and cook 6 hours or until chicken and vegetables are tender. Garnish, if desired.

You can substitute an extra ¼ cup chicken broth in place of the wine, if you prefer.

Slow-Cooker Red Beans and Rice

Slow-Cooker Red Beans and Rice

MAKES 10 servings • **HANDS-ON TIME:** 15 min. • **TOTAL TIME:** 7 hr., 15 min.

- 1 lb. dried red beans
- ¾ lb. smoked turkey sausage, thinly sliced
- 3 celery ribs, chopped
- 1 green bell pepper, chopped
- 1 red bell pepper, chopped
- 1 sweet onion, chopped
- 3 garlic cloves, minced
- 1 Tbsp. Creole seasoning
- Hot cooked long-grain rice
- Hot sauce (optional)
- Garnishes: finely chopped green onions, finely chopped red onion

1. Combine first 8 ingredients and 7 cups water in a 4-qt. slow cooker. Cover and cook on HIGH 7 hours or until beans are tender.
2. Serve red bean mixture with hot cooked rice, and, if desired, hot sauce. Garnish, if desired.

Vegetarian Red Beans and Rice: Substitute frozen meatless smoked sausage, thawed and thinly sliced, for turkey sausage.

Chicken-and-Wild Rice Hot Dish

MAKES 6 servings • **HANDS-ON TIME:** 15 min. • **TOTAL TIME:** 4 hr., 15 min.

- 4 skinned and boned chicken breasts (about 2 lb.)
- 1 cup chopped onion
- 1 cup chopped celery
- 5 garlic cloves, pressed
- 2 (6-oz.) packages uncooked long-grain and wild rice mix (we tested with Uncle Ben's)
- 2 (14-oz.) cans chicken broth with roasted garlic
- 2 (10¾ oz.) cans cream of mushroom soup
- 1 (8-oz.) package sliced fresh mushrooms
- 1 (8-oz.) can sliced water chestnuts, drained
- 1 cup chopped walnuts, toasted
- 2 Tbsp. butter

1. Brown chicken in a lightly greased large nonstick skillet over medium-high heat; remove from pan, and cut into ½-inch pieces. Add onion, celery, and garlic to pan; sauté 3 to 4 minutes or until tender.
2. Combine rice mix and next 6 ingredients in a 5-qt. slow cooker. Stir in chicken and vegetables.
3. Cover and cook on LOW 4 hours or until rice is tender and liquid is absorbed.

Slow-Cooker Turkey Chili

MAKES 4 to 6 servings • **HANDS-ON TIME:** 20 min. • **TOTAL TIME:** 6 hr., 20 min.

- 1¼ lb. lean ground turkey
- 1 large onion, chopped
- 1 garlic clove, minced
- 1 (1.25-oz.) envelope chili seasoning mix
- 1 (12-oz.) can beer
- 1½ cups frozen whole kernel corn, thawed
- 1 red bell pepper, chopped
- 1 green bell pepper, chopped
- 1 (28-oz.) can crushed tomatoes
- 1 (15-oz.) can black beans, drained and rinsed
- 1 (8-oz.) can tomato sauce
- ¾ tsp. salt
- Toppings: shredded Cheddar cheese, finely chopped red onion, sliced fresh jalapeño peppers

1. Cook first 4 ingredients in a large skillet over medium-high heat, stirring often, 8 minutes or until turkey crumbles and is no longer pink. Stir in beer, and cook 2 minutes, stirring occasionally. Spoon mixture into a 5½-qt. slow cooker; stir in corn and next 6 ingredients until well blended. Cover and cook on LOW 6 hours. Serve with desired toppings.

SHOPPER'S COMPANION

Slow-cooker prices range from $25 for a basic, two-temperature model to $125 or more for a programmable, multi-temperature model. Look for a stoneware insert. This dishwasher-, oven-, and microwave-safe insert makes cooking and cleaning a snap. Be sure to choose the right size. A standard 2½-qt. model is fine if you're cooking for 2; the 3½- to 5-qt. size serves a family of 4. Larger families need a slow cooker with at least a 6-qt. capacity.

Open-Faced Sloppy Toms

MAKES 6 to 8 servings • **HANDS-ON TIME:** 12 min. • **TOTAL TIME:** 6 hr., 12 min.

- 2 lb. ground turkey
- 2 (8-oz.) packages frozen chopped celery, onion, and bell pepper mix
- 1 Tbsp. jarred minced garlic
- 1 (15-oz.) can tomato sauce
- 1 (6-oz.) can tomato paste
- ⅓ cup firmly packed light brown sugar
- ¼ cup cider vinegar
- 2 Tbsp. Worcestershire sauce
- 2 tsp. paprika
- ½ tsp. chili powder
- ½ tsp. salt
- ½ tsp. freshly ground pepper
- 6 to 8 slices Texas toast
- Garnishes: finely chopped red onion, dill pickle slices

1. Brown first 3 ingredients in a large skillet over medium-high heat, stirring often, 10 minutes or until turkey crumbles and is no longer pink.
2. Meanwhile, combine tomato sauce and next 8 ingredients in a 5-qt. slow cooker. Stir turkey mixture into tomato sauce mixture. Cover and cook on LOW 6 hours.
3. Prepare Texas toast according to package directions. To serve, spoon turkey mixture over toast. Garnish, if desired.

SHOPPER'S COMPANION

Because Texas toast is thicker than regular bread, it pairs perfectly with extra-saucy dishes. It's great for soaking up all the extra liquid! There are several brands of frozen Texas toast available, and some supermarkets prepare their own versions (ready to toast). The choice is yours.

Seafood Pot Pie

MAKES 6 servings • **HANDS-ON TIME:** 15 min. • **TOTAL TIME:** 3 hr., 15 min.

- Parchment paper
- ¼ cup butter
- 1 cup chopped onion or 1 leek, thinly sliced
- 2 tsp. jarred minced garlic
- 1 (8-oz.) package sliced baby portobello mushrooms
- ¼ cup all-purpose flour
- 1 cup half-and-half
- 1 cup chicken broth
- 1 (11-oz.) package frozen baby broccoli blend
- 1 (1-lb.) cod fillet, cut into 2-inch pieces
- ½ lb. fresh lump crabmeat, drained and picked free of shell
- ½ tsp. salt
- ½ tsp. freshly ground pepper
- ½ (17.3-oz.) package frozen puff pastry sheets, thawed
- 1 egg yolk, beaten
- ¼ cup dry sherry

1. To make a template for pastry lid, place a 3½-qt. slow-cooker lid on parchment paper; trace lid shape. Remove lid. Cut out parchment-paper shape, and set aside.
2. Melt butter in a large skillet over medium-high heat. Add onion, garlic, and mushrooms; sauté 5 minutes. Whisk in flour until smooth. Cook 1 minute, whisking constantly. Gradually whisk in half-and-half and broth; cook over medium heat, whisking constantly, until thickened and bubbly. Transfer to a slow cooker. Stir in vegetables. Cover and cook on LOW 2 hours. Uncover and stir in cod, crabmeat, salt, and pepper. (Cooker will be almost full.) Cover and cook on HIGH 1 hour or until cod flakes with a fork.
3. Preheat oven to 400°. Roll out 1 pastry sheet on a lightly floured surface until smooth. Place parchment template on pastry, and cut out pastry using a paring knife. Place pastry on a parchment paper-lined baking sheet. Brush with egg yolk. Bake at 400° for 14 to 15 minutes. Stir sherry into pot pie. Top pot pie with pastry lid just before serving. Serve hot.

Prepare for rave reviews when you bake a puff pastry lid for this rich entrée and place it on top just before serving.

Shrimp Creole

Cook shrimp just until they turn pink and opaque.

MAKES 6 to 8 servings • **HANDS-ON TIME:** 8 min. • **TOTAL TIME:** 2 hr., 8 min.

- 4 bacon slices
- ½ cup chopped red bell pepper
- 1 (8-oz.) container refrigerated prechopped celery, onion, and bell pepper mix
- 3 garlic cloves, minced
- 2 Tbsp. chopped fresh parsley
- 1 tsp. Cajun seasoning
- 1 bay leaf
- ¼ tsp. salt
- ¼ tsp. freshly ground pepper
- 2 (14.5-oz.) cans stewed tomatoes
- 1½ lb. peeled and deveined large raw shrimp
- Hot cooked rice
- Garnish: chopped fresh parsley

1. Cook bacon over medium-high heat 4 to 5 minutes or until crisp; remove bacon, and drain on paper towels, reserving drippings in skillet. Crumble bacon. Add red bell pepper and celery mix to skillet; sauté 3 to 4 minutes or until tender. Add garlic; sauté 1 minute. Combine vegetable mixture, crumbled bacon, parsley, and next 5 ingredients in a lightly greased 4- to 5-qt. slow cooker. Cover and cook on HIGH 1 hour.

2. Stir in shrimp. Cover and cook on HIGH 45 minutes to 1 hour or until shrimp turn pink. Remove and discard bay leaf. Serve over hot cooked rice. Garnish, if desired.

Serve this classic Cajun dish with skewered grilled okra.

Seafood Gumbo

This recipe skips the tedious steps and hard-to-find spices of traditional gumbos without compromising any of the flavor. Serve over rice.

MAKES 6 servings • **HANDS-ON TIME:** 15 min. • **TOTAL TIME:** 3 hr., 20 min.

- **½ lb. sliced bacon, diced**
- **2 (8-oz.) containers refrigerated prechopped celery, onion, and bell pepper mix**
- **2 garlic cloves, minced**
- **2 cups chicken broth**
- **1 (14-oz.) can diced tomatoes**
- **2 Tbsp. Worcestershire sauce**
- **2 tsp. kosher salt**
- **1 tsp. dried thyme leaves**
- **¾ lb. large raw shrimp, peeled and deveined**
- **1 lb. fresh or frozen crabmeat**
- **2 cups frozen cut okra**

1. Cook bacon in a large skillet over medium heat until crisp. With a slotted spoon, transfer bacon to a 5-qt. slow cooker. Discard all but a thin coating of drippings in skillet. Add celery mix and garlic to skillet, and cook over medium heat, stirring frequently, until vegetables are tender, about 10 minutes.

2. Spoon vegetables into slow cooker; add broth, tomatoes, Worcestershire, salt, and thyme. Cover and cook on HIGH 2 hours. Add shrimp, crabmeat, and okra; reduce heat to LOW, and cook 1 hour. Serve over hot cooked rice.

How To Mince Garlic

Peel off papery skin from garlic, and slice off the tough ends with a knife. Make thin, lengthwise cuts through the clove, and then cut the strips crosswise.

Savory Italian Vegetable Bread Pudding

Savory Italian Vegetable Bread Pudding

MAKES 6 servings • **HANDS-ON TIME:** 8 min. • **TOTAL TIME:** 3 hr., 23 min.

- 1 Tbsp. olive oil
- 1 large zucchini, cubed
- 1 red bell pepper, chopped
- 1 small onion, chopped
- 6 large eggs
- 1 cup half-and-half
- 1½ tsp. Dijon mustard
- 1 tsp. dried Italian seasoning
- ½ tsp. salt
- ¼ tsp. pepper
- Texas toast, cut into 1-inch cubes
- 1 (9.5-oz.) package frozen mozzarella and Monterey Jack cheese
- 1 cup (4 oz.) shredded Italian six-cheese blend

1. Heat a large skillet over medium-high heat. Add oil. Sauté zucchini and next 2 ingredients in hot oil 5 minutes or until crisp-tender.
2. Whisk together eggs and next 5 ingredients.
3. Layer half of Texas toast in a lightly greased 5-qt. slow cooker; top with half of zucchini mixture and ½ cup cheese. Repeat layers. Pour egg mixture over all ingredients. Cover and cook on LOW 3 hours and 15 minutes or until set.

Slow-Cooker Cajun Succotash

MAKES 8 servings • **HANDS-ON TIME:** 6 min. • **TOTAL TIME:** 4 hr., 6 min.

- 2 cups frozen whole kernel corn
- 1 (14-oz.) can low-sodium fat-free vegetable broth
- 1½ tsp. Cajun seasoning
- 3 garlic cloves, minced
- 2 (16-oz.) cans red beans, drained and rinsed
- 1 (28-oz.) can diced tomatoes, undrained
- 1 (16-oz.) package frozen cut okra
- 1 large onion, chopped
- Hot cooked brown rice

1. Combine all ingredients, except rice, in a 5-qt. slow cooker. Cover and cook on LOW 4 hours. Serve over hot cooked brown rice.

Meatless Shepherd's Pie

MAKES 6 servings • **HANDS-ON TIME:** 8 min. • **TOTAL TIME:** 4 hr., 8 min.

- 2 (12-oz.) packages frozen meatless burger crumbles
- 2 Tbsp. all-purpose flour
- 1 (14.5-oz.) can diced tomatoes with basil, garlic, and oregano, undrained
- 1 (16-oz.) package frozen peas and carrots
- 1 tsp. dried minced onion
- 1 (24-oz.) package refrigerated sour cream and chive mashed potatoes
- 1 cup (4 oz.) shredded sharp Cheddar cheese

Garnish: fresh chives

1. Toss together burger crumbles and flour in a large bowl until crumbles are coated. Stir in tomatoes and next 2 ingredients. Spoon mixture into a lightly greased 4-qt. slow cooker.
2. Microwave potatoes 1 minute according to package directions; stir and spread over vegetable mixture in slow cooker. Cover and cook on LOW 4 hours. Increase heat to HIGH. Sprinkle cheese over potatoes; cover and cook 7 minutes or until cheese melts. Garnish, if desired.

SHORTCUT SECRET

Keep meatless burger crumbles in the freezer to make preparing quick, healthful meals a snap. They are ready to add to your recipes—no browning required.

Slow-Cooker Lasagna

MAKES 6 servings • **HANDS-ON TIME:** 15 min. • **TOTAL TIME:** 2 hr., 15 min.

- 1 (28-oz.) can diced tomatoes, drained
- 1 (28-oz.) jar chunky pasta sauce
- 3 garlic cloves, finely chopped
- ¼ cup fresh oregano, chopped
- ½ tsp. kosher salt
- ¾ tsp. pepper, divided
- 1 (16-oz.) container ricotta cheese
- ½ cup fresh flat-leaf parsley, chopped
- ½ cup (2 oz.) shredded Parmesan cheese
- 1 (12-oz.) package lasagna noodles
- 1 bunch Swiss chard, tough stems removed, and torn into large pieces
- 3 cups (12 oz.) shredded mozzarella cheese

1. In a medium bowl, combine tomatoes, sauce, garlic, oregano, salt, and ½ tsp. pepper. In another medium bowl, combine ricotta, parsley, Parmesan cheese, and remaining ¼ tsp. pepper. Spoon ⅓ cup tomato mixture into a 6-qt. oval slow cooker.

2. Top with a single layer of noodles, breaking them to fit as necessary. Add half of Swiss chard. Dollop with one-third of ricotta mixture and one-third of remaining tomato mixture. Sprinkle with one-third of mozzarella cheese. Add another layer of noodles, and repeat with other ingredients. Finish with a layer of noodles and remaining ricotta mixture, tomato mixture, and mozzarella. Cover and cook on LOW 2 to 3 hours or until noodles are tender.

Oval slow cookers work the best to accommodate lasagna.

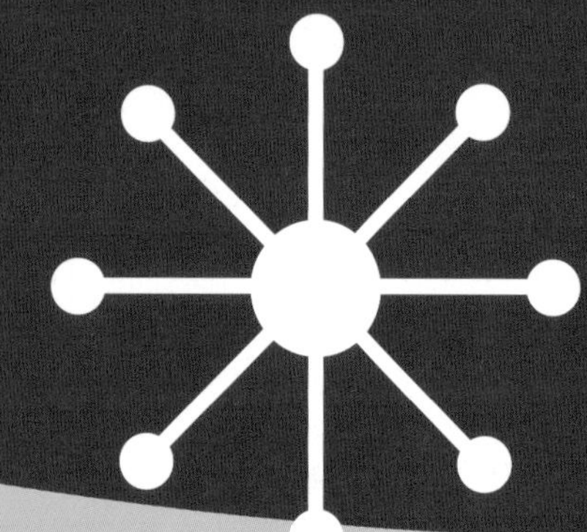

plugged in FOR SPEED

Pot Roast with Vegetables

Pot Roast with Vegetables

MAKES 4 to 6 servings • **HANDS-ON TIME:** 15 min. • **TOTAL TIME:** 1 hr., 15 min.

- 1 (3-lb.) boneless chuck roast, trimmed
- 2 Tbsp. vegetable oil
- 4 carrots, cut into 1-inch slices
- 3 potatoes, cut into 1½-inch cubes
- 1 medium onion, minced
- 1 (10½-oz.) can beef broth, undiluted
- 1 (8-oz.) can tomato sauce
- 1 cup dry red wine
- 1 tsp. sugar
- 1 tsp. hot sauce
- ¾ tsp. salt
- Garnish: parsley, freshly ground pepper

1. Brown roast on all sides in hot oil in a 6-qt. pressure cooker over medium-high heat. Add 3 cups water, carrots, and next 8 ingredients.
2. Cover with lid and seal securely; place pressure control on vent tube. Cook 1 hour with pressure control rocking slowly.
3. Remove from heat; run cold water over cooker to reduce pressure. Carefully remove lid. Garnish, if desired.

Roast with Onion-and-Mushroom Gravy

MAKES 4 to 6 servings • **HANDS-ON TIME:** 15 min. • **TOTAL TIME:** 1 hr., 5 min.

- 1 (2- to 3-lb.) boneless chuck roast, trimmed
- ½ tsp. pepper
- 1 (10¾-oz.) can cream of mushroom soup, undiluted
- 1 (1-oz.) envelope dry onion soup mix
- 2 beef bouillon cubes
- 2 Tbsp. cornstarch

1. Sprinkle roast evenly with pepper; place in a 6-qt. pressure cooker. Add 2 cups water, mushroom soup, and next 2 ingredients.
2. Cover with lid, and seal securely; place pressure control over vent tube. Cook over medium-high heat 20 minutes or until pressure control rocks back and forth quickly. Reduce heat to medium-low, and cook 20 more minutes.
3. Remove from heat; run cold water over cooker to reduce pressure. Carefully remove lid.
4. Remove roast, and keep warm. Stir together cornstarch and 2 Tbsp. water; add to liquid in cooker. Bring to a boil; cook 1 minute. Serve gravy with roast.

Corned Beef and Cabbage

MAKES 6 servings • **HANDS-ON TIME:** 15 min. • **TOTAL TIME:** 1 hr., 5 min.

- **1 (4-lb.) corned beef brisket**
- **3 Tbsp. pickling spice**
- **6 small red potatoes (about 2 lb.)**
- **1 head cabbage, cut into 6 wedges**
- **¾ cup sour cream**
- **2 Tbsp. prepared horseradish**

1. Combine brisket, pickling spice, and 2 cups water in a 6-qt. pressure cooker.
2. Cover with lid, and seal securely; place pressure control over vent tube. Cook over high heat until pressure control rocks back and forth quickly. Reduce heat until pressure control rocks occasionally; cook 50 minutes.
3. Remove from heat; run cold water over cooker to reduce pressure. Carefully remove lid.
4. Remove corned beef; keep warm. Add potatoes and cabbage to cooker. Cook as previously directed 5 minutes. Arrange potatoes and cabbage around corned beef.
5. Combine sour cream and horseradish; serve with corned beef, potatoes, and cabbage.

How To Prepare Cabbage

Start by removing and discarding the tough outer leaves from the head of the cabbage. Unlike its loose-leafed cousins, mustard and kale, cabbage is tightly wound so it doesn't pick up grit from the garden. Rinse under running water to clean it sufficiently, and then slice or chop it depending on the needs of the recipe.

Cincinnati Chili

company's coming

MAKES 6 to 8 servings • **HANDS-ON TIME:** 15 min. • **TOTAL TIME:** 30 min.

- 2 lb. ground round
- 2 (6-oz.) cans no-salt-added tomato paste
- 1 large onion, finely chopped
- 1 garlic clove, minced
- 2 large bay leaves
- 3 Tbsp. chili powder
- 1 Tbsp. ground cumin
- 2 tsp. ground allspice
- 1½ tsp. ground cinnamon
- 1 tsp. salt
- 1 tsp. black pepper
- 1 tsp. white wine vinegar
- 1 tsp. Worcestershire sauce
- ¼ tsp. ground red pepper
- Hot cooked spaghetti
- Shredded Cheddar cheese
- Chopped onion
- Oyster crackers

1. Combine ground round and 2 cups water in a 4-qt. pressure cooker; stir with a fork until thoroughly blended. Stir in tomato paste and next 12 ingredients.
2. Cover with lid, and seal securely; place pressure control over vent tube. Cook over high heat until pressure control rocks back and forth quickly. Reduce heat until pressure control rocks occasionally; cook 15 minutes.
3. Remove from heat; run cold water over cooker to reduce pressure. Carefully remove lid.
4. Remove and discard bay leaves. Serve chili over hot spaghetti, and top with cheese and onion. Serve with oyster crackers.

Speedy Lasagna

MAKES 6 servings • **HANDS-ON TIME:** 15 min. • **TOTAL TIME:** 1 hr.

- 1 lb. Italian sausage, casings removed
- 1 (26-oz.) jar spaghetti sauce with onions and roasted garlic
- 1 Tbsp. chopped fresh basil or 1 tsp. dried
- ½ tsp. pepper
- 6 no-cook lasagna noodles
- 2 cups ricotta cheese
- 2 cups (8 oz.) shredded mozzarella cheese
- ¾ cup grated Parmesan cheese

1. Crumble sausage into a plastic colander; place over a large microwave-safe bowl.
2. Microwave at HIGH 1 minute, and stir. Microwave at HIGH 3 to 3½ more minutes, stirring every 30 seconds, or until sausage is done and no longer pink. Drain well on paper towels. Discard drippings. Rinse and wipe bowl clean.
3. Stir together sausage, spaghetti sauce, basil, and pepper in a large bowl.
4. Spread one-third of sausage mixture in bottom of a lightly greased 11- x 7-inch microwave-safe baking dish; top with 3 noodles, 1 cup ricotta cheese, and 1 cup mozzarella cheese. Repeat layers once.
5. Top evenly with remaining sausage mixture and grated Parmesan cheese. Cover with heavy-duty plastic wrap, and microwave at MEDIUM (50% power) 30 to 35 minutes. Using an oven mitt, carefully lift 1 corner of plastic wrap to allow steam to escape, and let stand in microwave 5 minutes before serving.

Speedy Lasagna

Pork-and-Black Beans

You'll have a few tablespoons of salsa left that you can nibble on with chips as supper cooks, if desired. Double or triple the recipe if you'd like a larger yield; it will store several days in the refrigerator.

MAKES 1 serving • **HANDS-ON TIME:** 10 min. • **TOTAL TIME:** 20 min., including salsa

make ahead

- 1 (8.8-oz.) pouch ready-to-serve whole grain medley rice* (we tested with Uncle Ben's)
- ½ cup drained and rinsed canned black beans
- ¼ cup shredded fully cooked pork roast au jus (we tested with Hormel)
- 2 to 3 Tbsp. Cuban Salsa Verde

1. Remove ¾ cup rice from ready-to-serve pouch. Reserve remaining rice for another use.
2. Layer rice, beans, pork, and salsa, in this order, in a microwave-safe plastic container.
3. Cover with lid; lift 1 corner to allow steam to escape. Microwave at HIGH 1 to 2 minutes or until thoroughly heated. Stir before serving.

*1 (8.8-oz.) package ready-to-serve brown rice may be substituted.

Cuban Salsa Verde

MAKES ⅓ cup • **HANDS-ON TIME:** 10 min. • **TOTAL TIME:** 10 min.

- 1 cup loosely packed fresh cilantro
- 4 green onions, chopped
- 1 Tbsp. lime juice
- 1 Tbsp. extra virgin olive oil
- 2 garlic cloves
- 1 tsp. honey
- ¼ tsp. salt
- ¼ tsp. dried crushed red pepper

1. Process all ingredients in a food processor 30 seconds or until smooth, stopping to scrape down sides.

The microwave is a great tool for cooking a meal for one.

LTP
SOURCE
Perrier
SPARKLING NATURAL
MINERAL WATER
LOW MINERAL CONTENT
CONTAINS CARBONATED
MINERAL WATER
P11 29 07
E11 29 10
09:37 G

Sweet Chili-Lime Noodles with Vegetables

MAKES 1 serving • **HANDS-ON TIME:** 20 min. • **TOTAL TIME:** 25 min., including sauce

- 1 cup cooked whole grain spaghetti (2 oz. uncooked) (we tested with Mueller's)
- 2 cups shredded bok choy*
- ¼ cup grated carrot
- ¼ cup fresh snow peas
- Sweet Chili-Lime Sauce
- ¼ cup shredded cooked chicken (optional)

1. Place pasta, next 4 ingredients, and, if desired, chicken in a medium-size microwave-safe plastic container. Cover with lid, and shake to combine.
2. Lift 1 corner of lid to allow steam to escape. Microwave at HIGH 2 minutes or until vegetables are tender.
*2 cups shredded coleslaw mix or shredded cabbage may be substituted.

Sweet Chili-Lime Sauce

MAKES 3 Tbsp. • **HANDS-ON TIME:** 5 min. • **TOTAL TIME:** 5 min.

- 2 Tbsp. bottled sweet chili sauce
- 2 tsp. lime juice
- ½ tsp. grated fresh ginger
- ¼ tsp. minced garlic

1. Stir together all ingredients until blended.

This is the perfect dish to make when you need a quick dinner for 1 person. Or double the recipe to serve 2 people.

Cheese-and-Bacon Risotto

We used a 1,100-watt microwave oven and a 2½-liter glass bowl. We found that self-sealing plastic wraps, such as GLAD Press'n Seal, do not work in this application.

MAKES 4 servings • **HANDS-ON TIME:** 10 min. • **TOTAL TIME:** 32 min.

- ½ cup finely chopped sweet onion
- 2 Tbsp. butter
- 1 Tbsp. olive oil
- 1 garlic clove, minced
- 1 cup uncooked Arborio rice (short-grain) (we tested with Rice Select Italian-Style Rice)
- 2¾ cups low-sodium chicken broth
- ¼ cup dry white wine
- 1 cup freshly shredded extra-sharp Cheddar cheese
- 3 Tbsp. jarred diced pimiento, drained
- ¼ to ½ cup low-sodium chicken broth
- Salt and pepper to taste
- ¼ cup cooked and crumbled bacon
- 2 thinly sliced green onions

1. Stir together first 4 ingredients in a medium-size microwave-safe bowl. Microwave at HIGH 3 minutes. Stir in rice, and microwave at HIGH 2 minutes.

2. Stir in 2¾ cups broth and ¼ cup wine. Cover tightly with plastic wrap. (Do not vent.) Microwave at HIGH 9 minutes. Carefully swirl bowl without uncovering (to incorporate the mixture), and microwave at HIGH 8 minutes. Carefully remove and discard plastic wrap. Stir in cheese, pimiento, and ¼ cup chicken broth, stirring 30 seconds to 1 minute or until creamy. Add ¼ cup additional broth, 1 Tbsp. at a time, if necessary, for desired consistency. Season with salt and pepper to taste; sprinkle with crumbled bacon and sliced green onions just before serving.

SHOPPER'S COMPANION

Arborio rice is traditionally used for risotto because of its high starch content, which produces the creamy texture of the dish. Regular short-grain and medium-grain rice may be substituted in a pinch, but for best results, always look for imported Italian Arborio. (Check the rice aisle in your local supermarket; Arborio is often sold with other specialty rices.) Do not rinse risotto rice before cooking, as you'll wash away the starch.

Speedy Black Beans and Mexican Rice

MAKES 4 servings • **HANDS-ON TIME:** 12 min. • **TOTAL TIME:** 12 min.

30-minute special

- 2 (8.8-oz.) pouches ready-to-serve Spanish-style rice (we tested with Uncle Ben's)
- 2 (15-oz.) cans black beans, drained and rinsed
- 2 (4-oz.) cans chopped green chiles
- ¼ cup chopped fresh cilantro
- Toppings: sour cream, salsa, diced tomato, shredded Cheddar cheese

1. Prepare rice according to package directions.
2. Combine black beans and green chiles in a microwave-safe bowl. Microwave at HIGH 2 minutes or until thoroughly heated. Stir in rice and cilantro. Serve immediately with desired toppings.

This hearty dish is the perfect answer for a meatless main-dish choice.

meals
from the
GRILL

Grilled Pizza with Steak, Pear, and Arugula

company's coming

MAKES 4 servings • **HANDS-ON TIME:** 10 min. • **TOTAL TIME:** 50 min.

- Vegetable cooking spray
- ½ lb. flank steak
- Salt and pepper
- 1 Tbsp. olive oil
- 1½ tsp. white balsamic vinegar
- 1 (12-inch) prebaked pizza crust (we tested with Mama Mary's Thin and Crispy)
- 1 red Bartlett pear, peeled and sliced
- 1½ cups fresh arugula, divided
- ¼ cup crumbled Gorgonzola cheese
- Freshly cracked pepper

1. Coat cold cooking grate of grill with cooking spray, and place on grill. Preheat grill to 300° to 350° (medium) heat.
2. Season flank steak with salt and pepper.
3. Grill steak, covered with grill lid, 8 to 10 minutes on each side or to desired degree of doneness. Cover and let stand 10 minutes.
4. Meanwhile, whisk together oil and vinegar in a small bowl.
5. Cut steak diagonally across the grain into thin strips. Cut strips into bite-size pieces (about 1 cup).
6. Place pizza crust directly on hot cooking grate. Brush top of crust with oil mixture; layer with pear slices, 1 cup arugula, cheese, and beef strips.
7. Grill, covered with grill lid, 4 minutes. Rotate pizza one-quarter turn; grill, covered with grill lid, 5 to 6 more minutes or until thoroughly heated. Remove pizza from grill, and sprinkle with remaining ½ cup arugula and freshly cracked pepper.

SHORTCUT SECRET

On a rainy or cold evening or when you just don't have time to tend to the grill, it's nice to have the option of baking the pizza in the oven. To bake this pizza in the oven, assemble pizza as directed, and bake according to package directions for pizza crust.

Shrimp-Pesto Pizza

We found fresh pizza dough available behind the deli counter at the grocery store. If you're expecting a larger crowd, you can buy pizza dough in bulk from your local wholesale club or even a favorite pizza restaurant.

company's coming

MAKES 6 servings • **HANDS-ON TIME:** 37 min. • **TOTAL TIME:** 1 hr., including pesto

- Vegetable cooking spray
- 1 lb. unpeeled, large raw shrimp
- 1 large yellow onion, chopped
- 1 red bell pepper, chopped
- ¼ tsp. salt
- ¼ tsp. black pepper
- 1½ tsp. olive oil
- 1½ lb. bakery pizza dough
- All-purpose flour
- Plain yellow cornmeal
- ½ cup Garden Pesto*
- ¾ cup freshly grated Parmesan cheese

1. Coat cold cooking grate of grill with cooking spray, and place on grill. Preheat grill to 300° to 350° (medium) heat.
2. Peel shrimp, and slice in half lengthwise; devein, if desired.
3. Sauté onion, bell pepper, salt, and black pepper in ½ tsp. hot oil in a large skillet over medium heat 5 minutes or until tender. Transfer onion mixture to a large bowl. Sauté shrimp in remaining 1 tsp. hot oil 3 minutes or just until shrimp turn pink. Add shrimp to onion mixture, and toss.
4. Divide dough into 6 equal portions. Lightly sprinkle flour on a large surface. Roll each portion into a 6-inch round (about ¼ inch thick). Carefully transfer pizza dough rounds to a cutting board or baking sheet sprinkled with cornmeal.
5. Slide pizza dough rounds onto cooking grate of grill; spread Garden Pesto over rounds, and top with shrimp mixture. Sprinkle each with 2 Tbsp. Parmesan cheese.
6. Grill, covered with grill lid, 4 minutes. Rotate pizzas one-quarter turn, and grill, covered with grill lid, 5 to 6 more minutes or until pizza crusts are cooked. Serve immediately.
*Refrigerated store-bought pesto may be substituted.

Garden Pesto

MAKES 1¼ cups • **HANDS-ON TIME:** 10 min. • **TOTAL TIME:** 23 min.

- ¼ cup pine nuts
- ¼ cup chopped pecans
- 2½ cups firmly packed fresh basil leaves
- ½ cup chopped fresh parsley
- 2 garlic cloves, chopped
- ⅓ cup olive oil
- ¾ cup (3 oz.) shredded Parmesan cheese
- ⅓ cup olive oil

1. Preheat oven to 350°. Bake pine nuts and pecans in a single layer in a shallow pan 8 minutes or until toasted and fragrant. Let cool 5 minutes. Process basil leaves, parsley, garlic, and ⅓ cup olive oil in a food processor until a coarse paste forms. Add nuts and Parmesan cheese, and process until blended. With processor running, pour ⅓ cup olive oil through food chute in a slow, steady stream; process until smooth. Cover and chill up to 5 days.

Grilled Shrimp-and-Green Bean Salad

MAKES 4 to 6 servings • **HANDS-ON TIME:** 38 min. • **TOTAL TIME:** 1 hr., 18 min., including vinaigrette

- 8 (12-inch) wooden skewers
- 2 lb. peeled, medium-size raw shrimp
- Basil Vinaigrette, divided
- 1½ lb. fresh green beans, trimmed
- 6 cooked bacon slices, crumbled
- 1⅓ cups (5½ oz.) shredded Parmesan cheese
- ¾ cup chopped roasted, salted almonds
- Cornbread (optional)

1. Soak wooden skewers in water 30 minutes.
2. Meanwhile, combine shrimp and ¾ cup Basil Vinaigrette in a large zip-top plastic freezer bag; seal and chill 15 minutes, turning occasionally.
3. Preheat grill to 350° to 400° (medium-high) heat.
4. Cook green beans in boiling salted water to cover 4 minutes or until crisp-tender; drain. Plunge into ice water to stop the cooking process; drain, pat dry, and place in a large bowl.
5. Remove shrimp from marinade, discarding marinade. Thread shrimp onto skewers.
6. Grill shrimp, covered with grill lid, 2 minutes on each side or just until shrimp turn pink. Remove shrimp from skewers, and toss with green beans, crumbled bacon, Parmesan cheese, roasted almonds, and remaining ¾ cup Basil Vinaigrette. Serve over hot cooked cornbread, if desired.

Basil Vinaigrette

MAKES 1½ cups • **HANDS-ON TIME:** 10 min. • **TOTAL TIME:** 10 min.

- ½ cup chopped fresh basil
- ½ cup balsamic vinegar
- 4 large shallots, minced
- 3 garlic cloves, minced
- 1 Tbsp. brown sugar
- 1 tsp. seasoned pepper
- ½ tsp. salt
- 1 cup olive oil

1. Whisk together first 7 ingredients until blended. Gradually add olive oil, whisking constantly until blended.

Spicy Glazed Shrimp Kabobs

Serve these party-ready grilled kabobs over your favorite rice or pasta.

MAKES 4 to 6 servings • **HANDS-ON TIME:** 45 min. • **TOTAL TIME:** 1 hr., 15 min.

- **16 (7- to 8-inch) wooden skewers**
- **2 Tbsp. honey**
- **2 Tbsp. spicy brown mustard**
- **1½ lb. peeled, jumbo-size raw shrimp with tails**
- **1 Tbsp. Caribbean jerk seasoning**
- **2 Tbsp. olive oil**
- **¼ tsp. salt**
- **3 yellow squash, cut into ¼- to ½-inch slices**
- **2 zucchini, cut into ¼- to ½-inch slices**
- **1 red bell pepper, cut into 1½-inch pieces**
- **1 Tbsp. olive oil**
- **Salt and pepper to taste**

1. Soak wooden skewers in water 30 minutes. Stir together honey and spicy brown mustard. Toss shrimp with Caribbean jerk seasoning, 2 Tbsp. olive oil, and ¼ tsp. salt. Thread onto 8 skewers. Thread squash slices, zucchini slices, and red bell pepper pieces onto remaining 8 skewers. Brush vegetable kabobs with 1 Tbsp. olive oil; sprinkle with salt and pepper to taste.
2. Preheat grill to 350° to 400° (medium-high) heat.
3. Grill vegetable kabobs, covered with grill lid, 15 minutes or until tender, turning occasionally. Grill shrimp, covered with grill lid, 2 minutes on each side or just until shrimp turn pink. Baste shrimp with honey mixture. Serve immediately.

How To Cut Bell Peppers

If you plan to use the peppers within a day or two, keep them at room temperature for better flavor. You can also store them in a plastic bag in the fridge for up to a week. Be sure to wash and cut the peppers just before using them. Use a knife to slice the pepper in half, then cut it into quarters. Pull the stems and seeds away, and slice each quarter to desired size.

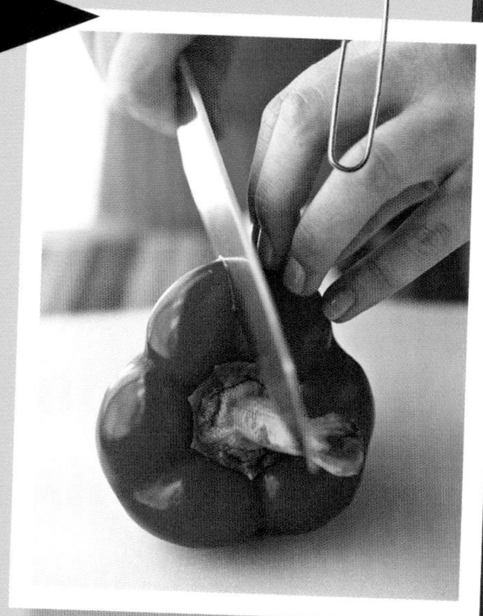

Shredded Grilled Tilapia Tacos

MAKES 6 servings • **HANDS-ON TIME:** 10 min. • **TOTAL TIME:** 39 min., including slaw and salsa

- 1 Tbsp. ground chipotle seasoning
- 1½ tsp. ground cumin
- ½ tsp. salt
- 6 (6-oz.) tilapia fillets
- 2 Tbsp. olive oil
- 1 tsp. lime zest
- 2 Tbsp. fresh lime juice
- Vegetable cooking spray
- 12 corn tortillas
- Sweet-and-Spicy Slaw
- Fruity Black Bean Salsa
- Fresh lime wedges

1. Preheat grill to 350° to 400° (medium-high) heat. Combine first 3 ingredients. Rub seasoning mixture evenly over fillets.
2. Stir together oil, lime zest, and juice; rub over fillets.
3. Arrange fillets in a grill basket coated with cooking spray.
4. Grill 3 minutes on each side or just until fish begins to flake with a fork. Cool slightly. Shred fish. Spoon 2 to 3 Tbsp. fish into each tortilla; top with Sweet-and-Spicy Slaw and Fruity Black Bean Salsa. Serve with a squeeze of fresh lime juice.

Sweet-and-Spicy Slaw

MAKES 12 servings • **HANDS-ON TIME:** 8 min. • **TOTAL TIME:** 8 min.

- 1 cup reduced-fat sour cream
- 2 Tbsp. rice wine vinegar
- 2 Tbsp. pineapple or orange marmalade
- ½ tsp. salt
- ¼ to ½ tsp. ground chipotle seasoning
- 1 (16-oz.) package cabbage slaw mix

1. Whisk together first 5 ingredients in a medium glass bowl until blended. Add slaw mix, tossing to coat. Cover and chill until ready to serve.

Fruity Black Bean Salsa

MAKES 7 servings • **HANDS-ON TIME:** 15 min. • **TOTAL TIME:** 15 min.

- 1 (15-oz.) can black beans, drained and rinsed
- 1 small papaya, peeled, seeded, and cut into ½-inch cubes
- ½ red or green bell pepper, seeded and chopped
- 1 large ripe avocado, cut into ½-inch cubes
- 2 jalapeño peppers, seeded and minced
- ¼ cup chopped fresh cilantro
- 1 tsp. lemon zest
- 2 Tbsp. fresh lemon juice
- 1 Tbsp. honey
- ½ tsp. salt

1. Combine black beans and next 5 ingredients in a glass bowl. Whisk together lemon zest and next 3 ingredients in a small bowl; drizzle over bean mixture. Toss gently to coat.
2. Cover and chill until ready to serve.

Citrus Shrimp Tacos

Soak wooden skewers in water at least 30 minutes before grilling to keep them from burning.

MAKES 6 to 8 servings • **HANDS-ON TIME:** 30 min. • **TOTAL TIME:** 1 hr., 45 min., including salsa and sauce

- 2 lb. unpeeled, large raw shrimp
- 20 (12-inch) wooden skewers
- 2 Tbsp. Southwest seasoning (we tested with Emeril's Southwest Essence)
- 3 garlic cloves, minced
- ⅓ cup lime juice
- 3 Tbsp. lemon juice
- 16 (8-inch) soft taco-size flour tortillas, warmed
- 1 head iceberg lettuce, finely shredded
- 1 head radicchio, finely shredded
- Grilled Corn Salsa
- Southwest Cream Sauce
- Garnish: fresh cilantro leaves

1. Peel shrimp; devein, if desired. Thread shrimp onto skewers.
2. Preheat grill to 350° to 400° (medium-high) heat. Combine Southwest seasoning and garlic in a long shallow dish; add lime juice, lemon juice, and shrimp, turning to coat. Cover and chill 10 minutes. Remove shrimp from marinade, discarding marinade.
3. Grill shrimp, without grill lid, 2 to 3 minutes on each side or just until shrimp turn pink. Remove shrimp from skewers. Serve in warm tortillas with next 4 ingredients. Garnish, if desired.

Grilled Corn Salsa

MAKES 6 cups • **HANDS-ON TIME:** 25 min. • **TOTAL TIME:** 55 min.

- 3 ears fresh corn, husks removed
- Vegetable cooking spray
- 1 tsp. salt
- ½ tsp. black pepper
- 3 medium tomatoes, seeded and chopped
- 2 jalapeño peppers, seeded and minced
- 2 (15-oz.) cans black beans, drained and rinsed
- ¾ cup chopped fresh cilantro
- ⅓ cup fresh lime juice
- 2 Tbsp. chopped fresh mint
- 2 avocados
- Tortilla chips (optional)

1. Preheat grill to 350° to 400° (medium-high) heat. Lightly coat corn cobs with cooking spray. Sprinkle with salt and black pepper.
2. Grill corn, covered with grill lid, 15 to 20 minutes or until golden brown, turning every 5 minutes. Remove from grill; cool 15 minutes.
3. Hold each grilled cob upright on a cutting board; carefully cut downward, cutting kernels from cob.
4. Discard cobs; place kernels in a large bowl. Gently stir in tomatoes and next 5 ingredients. Serve immediately, or cover and chill until ready to serve.
5. If chilled, let corn mixture stand at room temperature 30 minutes. Peel and chop avocados; toss with corn mixture just before serving. Serve with tortilla chips, if desired.

Southwest Cream Sauce

MAKES about 2 cups • **HANDS-ON TIME:** 10 min. • **TOTAL TIME:** 10 min.

- 1 (16-oz.) container sour cream
- 1 garlic clove, minced
- 2 Tbsp. finely chopped red onion
- 1 tsp. chili powder
- ½ tsp. ground cumin
- ½ tsp. ground red pepper
- ¼ tsp. salt
- 2 Tbsp. chopped fresh cilantro
- 2 Tbsp. fresh lime juice

1. Whisk together first 7 ingredients. Whisk in cilantro and lime juice until smooth. Cover and chill until ready to serve.

Shrimp Burgers with Sweet 'n' Spicy Tartar Sauce

Recipes for shrimp burgers, a favorite food of Southern shrimping towns, are often a big secret. Here we divulge our version, which is chunky and spicy with some Cajun flair.

MAKES 4 servings • **HANDS-ON TIME:** 35 min. • **TOTAL TIME:** 2 hr., 40 min., including sauce

- 1¼ lb. unpeeled, medium-size raw shrimp
- Vegetable cooking spray
- 1 large egg, lightly beaten
- 1 Tbsp. mayonnaise
- 2 tsp. lemon juice
- ½ tsp. salt
- ⅛ tsp. ground red pepper
- 3 Tbsp. finely chopped celery
- 2 Tbsp. chopped green onions
- 1 Tbsp. chopped fresh parsley
- 1¼ cups crushed cornbread crackers (about 1 sleeve or 24 crackers; we tested with Keebler Town House Bistro Corn Bread Crackers)
- 4 Kaiser rolls with poppy seeds, split
- Sweet 'n' Spicy Tartar Sauce
- 4 Bibb lettuce leaves
- Garnish: grilled lemon halves

1. Peel shrimp; devein, if desired. Cut each shrimp into thirds.
2. Line a 15- x 10-inch jelly-roll pan with aluminum foil. Coat foil with cooking spray.
3. Stir together egg and next 4 ingredients until blended; stir in celery, green onions, and parsley.
4. Fold in shrimp and cracker crumbs. (Mixture will be very thick.) Shape into 4 (4-inch-wide, 1-inch-thick) patties. Place patties on prepared pan. Cover and chill 1 to 24 hours. Transfer to freezer, and freeze 30 minutes.
5. Coat cold cooking grate of grill with cooking spray, and place on grill. Preheat grill to 350° to 400° (medium-high) heat. Grill burgers, covered with grill lid, 4 to 5 minutes or until burgers lift easily from cooking grate using a large spatula. Turn burgers, and grill 4 to 5 minutes or until shrimp turn pink and burgers are cooked through and lightly crisp.
6. Grill rolls, cut sides down, 1 to 2 minutes or until lightly toasted. Serve burgers on toasted rolls with Sweet 'n' Spicy Tartar Sauce and lettuce. Garnish, if desired.

Sweet 'n' Spicy Tartar Sauce:

MAKES about 1 cup • **HANDS-ON TIME:** 5 min. • **TOTAL TIME:** 35 min.

- 1 cup mayonnaise
- 2 Tbsp. chopped fresh parsley
- 2 Tbsp. horseradish
- 1½ tsp. Cajun seasoning (we tested with McCormick)
- 1½ tsp. lemon juice
- ¼ tsp. paprika

1. Stir together all ingredients in a bowl. Cover and chill 30 minutes to 24 hours.

Greek Turkey Burgers

MAKES 4 servings • **HANDS-ON TIME:** 25 min. • **TOTAL TIME:** 25 min.

- **1⅓ lb. ground turkey breast**
- **1 (4-oz.) package crumbled feta cheese**
- **¼ cup finely chopped red onion**
- **1 tsp. dried oregano**
- **1 tsp. lemon zest**
- **½ tsp. salt**
- **Vegetable cooking spray**
- **½ cup grated English cucumber**
- **1 (6-oz.) container fat-free Greek yogurt**
- **1 Tbsp. chopped fresh mint**
- **½ tsp. salt**
- **4 French hamburger buns, split and toasted**
- **Toppings: lettuce leaves, tomato slices, thinly sliced cucumber**
- **Garnish: pepperoncini salad peppers**

1. Stir together first 6 ingredients. Shape mixture into 4 (½-inch-thick) patties.
2. Heat a grill pan over medium-high heat. Coat grill pan with cooking spray. Add patties; cook 5 minutes on each side or until done.
3. Stir together cucumber, yogurt, mint, and ½ tsp. salt in a small bowl. Serve burgers on buns with cucumber sauce and desired toppings. Garnish, if desired.

Bacon-Wrapped Barbecue Burgers

This dressed-up burger is a true crowd-pleaser.

kids' favorite

MAKES 4 servings • **HANDS-ON TIME:** 39 min. • **TOTAL TIME:** 54 min.

- 8 bacon slices
- 1 (4.5-oz.) jar sliced mushrooms, drained and chopped
- ½ cup chopped Vidalia or sweet onion
- 2 tsp. olive oil
- ½ cup bottled honey barbecue sauce, divided (we tested with Kraft)
- 1½ lb. ground beef
- Wooden picks
- ¼ tsp. salt
- 4 sesame seed hamburger buns, toasted

1. Arrange bacon on a paper towel-lined microwave-safe plate; cover with a paper towel. Microwave bacon at HIGH 2 minutes or until edges begin to crinkle and bacon is partially cooked.
2. Sauté mushrooms and onion in hot oil in a small nonstick skillet over medium heat 4 to 5 minutes or until tender and liquid is absorbed. Remove from heat, and stir in 2 Tbsp. barbecue sauce.
3. Preheat grill to 350° to 400° (medium-high) heat. Shape ground beef into 8 (5-inch) thin patties. Place 2 Tbsp. mushroom mixture in center of each of 4 patties. Top with remaining patties, pressing edges to seal. Shape into 4-inch patties. Wrap sides of each patty with 2 bacon slices, overlapping ends of each slice. Secure bacon using wooden picks. Sprinkle patties with salt. Cover and chill 10 minutes.
4. Grill patties, covered with grill lid, 5 to 6 minutes on 1 side. Turn and baste with half of remaining barbecue sauce. Grill 5 to 6 more minutes or until beef is no longer pink in center. Turn and baste with remaining barbecue sauce. Remove from grill, and let stand 5 minutes. Remove wooden picks. Serve burgers on buns, and top with remaining mushroom mixture.

If you use beef from your freezer, make sure it has been wrapped and frozen for 3 months or less for best flavor.

Sweet-and-Savory Burgers

MAKES 8 servings • **HANDS-ON TIME:** 25 min. • **TOTAL TIME:** 4 hr., 25 min.

- ¼ cup soy sauce
- 2 Tbsp. light corn syrup
- 1 Tbsp. fresh lemon juice
- ½ tsp. ground ginger
- ¼ tsp. garlic powder
- 2 green onions, thinly sliced
- 2 lb. ground beef
- ¼ cup chili sauce
- ¼ cup hot red pepper jelly
- 8 hamburger buns, toasted
- Toppings: grilled sweet onion and pineapple slices

1. Stir together first 6 ingredients. Reserve 3 Tbsp. mixture; cover and chill. Pour remaining soy sauce mixture into a shallow pan or baking dish.
2. Shape beef into 8 (½-inch-thick) patties; place in a single layer in soy sauce mixture in pan, turning to coat. Cover and chill 4 hours.
3. Preheat grill to 350° to 400° (medium-high) heat. Remove patties from marinade, discarding marinade. Grill patties, covered with grill lid, 5 minutes on each side or until beef is no longer pink in center, basting occasionally with reserved 3 Tbsp. soy sauce mixture.
4. Stir together chili sauce and jelly. Serve burgers on buns with chili sauce mixture and desired toppings.

Press your thumb into centers of patties before grilling for burgers that cook up flat, rather than domed, across the top.

Molasses-Balsamic Steak Kabobs with Green Tomatoes

company's coming

MAKES 4 to 6 servings • **HANDS-ON TIME:** 38 min. • **TOTAL TIME:** 1 hr., 8 min.

- 8 (12-inch) wooden or metal skewers
- 1 (1½-lb.) boneless sirloin steak, trimmed and cut into 1½-inch pieces
- 4 small, firm peaches, quartered
- 2 medium-size green tomatoes, cut into eighths
- 2 medium-size red onions, cut into eighths
- 2 tsp. seasoned salt
- 2 tsp. pepper
- ½ cup molasses
- ¼ cup balsamic vinegar

1. Soak wooden skewers in water 30 minutes.
2. Preheat grill to 350° to 400° (medium-high) heat. Thread steak and next 3 ingredients alternately onto skewers, leaving a ¼-inch space between pieces. Sprinkle kabobs with seasoned salt and pepper. Stir together molasses and vinegar.
3. Grill kabobs, covered with grill lid, 4 minutes on each side. Baste with half of molasses mixture, and grill 2 minutes. Turn, baste with remaining half of molasses mixture, and grill 2 more minutes or until done.

Use basting brushes made of natural bristles to dab on marinades and sauces.

Greek-Style Beef and Vegetables

This recipe calls for you to grill twice as much meat as you will need, so save half for another recipe later in the week.

MAKES 4 servings • **HANDS-ON TIME:** 20 min. • **TOTAL TIME:** 54 min., including sauce

- 2 lb. (1-inch-thick) boneless top sirloin steak
- 3 Tbsp. olive oil, divided
- 2 tsp. kosher salt, divided
- 1 tsp. freshly ground pepper, divided
- 6 medium-size yellow squash, cut in half
- 1 red onion, cut into ½-inch-thick slices
- 1 lemon, cut in half
- 1 (10-oz.) box plain couscous
- ½ (4-oz.) package crumbled feta cheese
- Chunky Cucumber-Mint Sauce

1. Preheat grill to 350° to 400° (medium-high) heat. Rub steak with 1 Tbsp. oil, 1½ tsp. kosher salt, and ¾ tsp. pepper.
2. Brush squash and onion with remaining 2 Tbsp. oil; sprinkle with remaining ½ tsp. kosher salt and ¼ tsp. pepper.
3. Grill steak and vegetables, covered with grill lid, 5 to 7 minutes on each side or until steak reaches desired degree of doneness and vegetables are tender. Remove steak and vegetables from grill; squeeze juice from lemon over steak and vegetables. Cover steak and vegetables with aluminum foil, and let stand 10 minutes.
4. Meanwhile, prepare couscous according to package directions.
5. Cut steak across the grain into thin slices. Cover and chill half of sliced steak (about 1 lb.) up to 2 days. Top couscous with vegetables; sprinkle with feta cheese. Serve with remaining half of steak and Chunky Cucumber-Mint Sauce.

Chunky Cucumber-Mint Sauce

MAKES 1¾ cups • **HANDS-ON TIME:** 10 min. • **TOTAL TIME:** 10 min.

- 1 cup plain yogurt
- 3 Tbsp. sour cream
- 1 small cucumber, peeled, seeded, and chopped
- 4 tsp. chopped fresh mint
- Salt and pepper to taste

1. Stir together all ingredients.

Beef Fajitas with Pico de Gallo

This tasty favorite cooks on an indoor grill. When using an outdoor gas or charcoal grill, grill steaks, covered with grill lid, at 350° to 400° (medium-high heat) 8 minutes. Turn and grill 5 more minutes or to desired degree of doneness. Proceed as directed.

MAKES 6 servings • **HANDS-ON TIME:** 20 min. • **TOTAL TIME:** 9 hr., 45 min., including Pico de Gallo

- **1 (8-oz.) bottle zesty Italian dressing**
- **3 Tbsp. fajita seasoning (we tested with McCormick)**
- **2 (1-lb.) flank steaks**
- **12 (6-inch) flour tortillas, warmed**
- **Shredded Cheddar cheese**
- **Pico de Gallo**
- **Garnishes: lime wedges and fresh cilantro sprigs**

1. Combine Italian dressing and fajita seasoning in a shallow dish or zip-top plastic bag; add steak. Cover or seal, and chill 8 hours, turning occasionally. Remove steak from marinade, discarding marinade.

2. Preheat a two-sided contact indoor electric grill according to manufacturer's instructions on HIGH. Place steaks on food grate, close lid, and grill 10 minutes (medium-rare) or to desired degree of doneness. Remove steaks, and let stand 5 minutes.

3. Cut steaks diagonally across the grain into very thin slices, and serve with tortillas, cheese, and Pico de Gallo. Garnish, if desired.

Pico de Gallo

MAKES about 3 cups • **HANDS-ON TIME:** 25 min. • **TOTAL TIME:** 1 hr., 25 min.

- **1 pt. grape tomatoes, chopped***
- **1 green bell pepper, chopped**
- **1 red bell pepper, chopped**
- **1 avocado, peeled and chopped**
- **½ medium-size red onion, chopped**
- **½ cup chopped fresh cilantro**
- **1 garlic clove, pressed**
- **¾ tsp. salt**
- **½ tsp. ground cumin**
- **½ tsp. lime zest**
- **¼ cup fresh lime juice**

1. Stir together all ingredients; cover and chill 1 hour.

*2 large tomatoes, chopped, may be substituted.

Pork Kabobs with Green Tomatoes and Plums

MAKES 4 to 6 servings • **HANDS-ON TIME:** 38 min. • **TOTAL TIME:** 1 hr., 8 min.

- 8 (12-inch) wooden or metal skewers
- 1 (1.5-lb.) package pork tenderloin, trimmed and cut into 1½-inch pieces
- 4 large plums, quartered
- 2 medium-size green tomatoes, cut into eighths
- 2 medium-size red onions, cut into eighths
- 2 tsp. seasoned salt
- 2 tsp. pepper
- ½ cup molasses
- ¼ cup balsamic vinegar

1. Soak wooden skewers in water 30 minutes.
2. Preheat grill to 350° to 400° (medium-high) heat. Thread pork and next 3 ingredients alternately onto skewers, leaving a ¼-inch space between pieces. Sprinkle kabobs with seasoned salt and pepper. Stir together molasses and vinegar.
3. Grill kabobs, covered with grill lid, 12 minutes, turning after 6 minutes. Baste kabobs with half of molasses mixture, and grill 3 minutes. Turn kabobs, baste with remaining half of molasses mixture, and grill 3 more minutes or until done.

SHORTCUT SECRET

Save time by using metal skewers rather than wooden skewers. Wooden skewers need to soak for 30 minutes before you can use them, while metal skewers can go right on the grill.

Spicy Grilled Pork Tenderloin with Blackberry Sauce

MAKES 6 to 8 servings • **HANDS-ON TIME:** 15 min. • **TOTAL TIME:** 40 min.

- 2 (¾-lb.) pork tenderloins
- 1 Tbsp. olive oil
- 1½ Tbsp. Caribbean jerk seasoning
- 1 tsp. salt
- ⅔ cup seedless blackberry preserves
- ¼ cup Dijon mustard
- 2 Tbsp. rum or orange juice
- 1 Tbsp. orange zest
- 1 Tbsp. grated fresh ginger
- Mixed salad greens
- Chopped mango
- Blackberries

1. Preheat grill to 350° to 400° (medium-high) heat. Remove silver skin from tenderloins, leaving a thin layer of fat. Brush tenderloins with oil, and rub with seasoning and salt.
2. Grill tenderloins, covered with grill lid, 10 minutes on each side or until a meat thermometer inserted into thickest portion registers 155°. Remove from grill, and let stand 10 minutes.
3. Meanwhile, whisk together blackberry preserves and next 4 ingredients in a small saucepan, and cook over low heat, whisking constantly, 5 minutes or until thoroughly heated.
4. Cut pork diagonally into thin slices, and arrange on a serving platter with mixed salad greens, mangoes, and blackberries; drizzle with warm sauce.

How To Grate Fresh Ginger

Use a vegetable peeler to remove the tough skin of ginger and reveal the flesh. Rub a peeled piece of ginger across a fine grater such as a Microplane®.

Grilled Sausages

MAKES 4 servings • **HANDS-ON TIME:** 36 min. • **TOTAL TIME:** 2 hr., 21 min., including relish

- **4 fresh pork sausages**
- **2 (12-oz.) bottles lager beer**
- **2 (8-inch) hoagie rolls**
- **Sweet Pepper-Onion Relish**

1. Preheat grill to 350° to 400° (medium-high) heat. Bring sausages and beer to a boil in a Dutch oven over medium-high heat. Cover, remove from heat, and let stand 10 minutes. Drain.
2. Cut a ½-inch-deep wedge from top of each roll. Reserve wedges for another use, if desired. Cut rolls in half crosswise.
3. Grill sausages, covered with grill lid, 8 to 10 minutes on each side or to desired degree of doneness.
4. Place 1 sausage in each roll half. Spoon desired amount of Sweet Pepper-Onion Relish over each sausage.

Sweet Pepper-Onion Relish

MAKES 5 cups • **HANDS-ON TIME:** 20 min. • **TOTAL TIME:** 1 hr., 35 min.

- **2 red bell peppers, seeded and diced**
- **2 yellow bell peppers, seeded and diced**
- **1 large yellow onion, diced**
- **3 garlic cloves, minced**
- **2 Tbsp. olive oil**
- **2 Tbsp. balsamic vinegar**
- **1 tsp. salt**
- **½ tsp. dried thyme**
- **½ tsp. dried crushed red pepper**

1. Preheat oven to 400°. Stir together all ingredients, and pour into an 11- x 7-inch baking dish. Bake 45 minutes or until soft, stirring every 5 minutes. Transfer pepper mixture and any liquid to a bowl. Let cool 30 minutes or to room temperature. Store in an airtight container in refrigerator up to 3 days.

SHOPPER'S COMPANION

You may substitute chicken for the pork sausages. We tested with Johnsonville Stadium Style Brats and Yuengling Traditional Lager, but you may use 4½ cups water for the beer, if you prefer.

Spicy Thai Chicken Kabobs

Stir up a superfast peanut sauce and marinate the chicken before you head out for the day. The remaining ingredients can be put together quickly when you get home from work.

MAKES 4 to 6 servings • **HANDS-ON TIME:** 20 min. • **TOTAL TIME:** 9 hr., 6 min.

- ½ cup creamy peanut butter
- ½ cup lite soy sauce
- ¼ cup firmly packed light brown sugar
- 1 Tbsp. lime zest
- 1 tsp. dried crushed red pepper
- 1½ lb. skinned and boned chicken breasts, cut into 1-inch pieces
- 8 (12-inch) wooden or metal skewers
- 1 bunch green onions, cut into 2-inch pieces
- 1 large red bell pepper, cut into 1-inch pieces
- 1 large yellow bell pepper, cut into 1-inch pieces
- 32 fresh snow peas
- 16 basil leaves

1. Whisk together first 5 ingredients and ½ cup water in a large shallow dish or zip-top plastic freezer bag; reserve ¾ cup. Add chicken to dish or bag, turning to coat. Cover or seal, and chill 8 hours, turning occasionally.
2. Soak wooden skewers in water 30 minutes.
3. Preheat grill to 350° to 400° (medium-high) heat. Remove chicken from marinade, discarding marinade. Thread chicken, onions, and next 4 ingredients alternately onto wooden skewers, leaving a ¼-inch space between pieces.
4. Grill kabobs, covered with grill lid, 6 to 8 minutes on each side or until done. Remove from grill, and baste with reserved ¾ cup marinade.

Spicy Thai Pork Kabobs: Substitute 1 (1.5-lb.) package pork tenderloin, trimmed, for chicken. Proceed with recipe as directed.

Herb-Grilled Chicken with Watermelon-Feta Salad

MAKES 4 servings • **HANDS-ON TIME:** 20 min. • **TOTAL TIME:** 1 hr., 12 min., including salad

- 3 Tbsp. fresh lemon juice
- 3 Tbsp. vegetable oil
- ¼ cup chopped fresh flat-leaf parsley
- 1 tsp. dried oregano
- ¾ tsp. salt
- ½ tsp. ground cumin
- ½ tsp. pepper
- 4 skinned and boned chicken breasts
- Vegetable cooking spray
- Watermelon-Feta Salad

1. Whisk together first 7 ingredients in a shallow dish; remove and reserve 2 Tbsp. marinade for Watermelon-Feta Salad. Add chicken to dish; cover and chill 30 minutes.
2. Coat cold cooking grate of grill with cooking spray; place on grill. Preheat grill to 300° to 350° (medium) heat.
3. Remove chicken from marinade, discarding marinade. Grill chicken 6 minutes on each side or until done. Serve with Watermelon-Feta Salad.

Watermelon-Feta Salad

MAKES 3 cups • **HANDS-ON TIME:** 10 min. • **TOTAL TIME:** 10 min.

- 1½ cups diced seedless watermelon
- ¾ cup diced cucumber
- ¼ cup coarsely chopped pitted kalamata olives
- ¼ cup diced red onion
- 2 Tbsp. reserved marinade
- ¼ cup crumbled feta cheese

1. Place first 5 ingredients in a large bowl; gently toss. Sprinkle with feta cheese.

Margarita-Marinated Chicken with Mango Salsa

MAKES 6 servings • **HANDS-ON TIME:** 22 min. • **TOTAL TIME:** 2 hr., 32 min., including salsa

- 2 large limes
- 2 cups liquid margarita mix
- 1 cup vegetable oil
- 1 cup chopped fresh cilantro
- 2 tsp. salt
- ½ tsp. ground red pepper
- 3 Tbsp. tequila (optional)
- 6 skinned and boned chicken breasts
- 2 cups uncooked long-grain white rice
- Vegetable cooking spray
- Mango Salsa

1. Cut limes in half. Squeeze juice into a shallow dish or large zip-top plastic freezer bag; add squeezed lime halves to juice. Add margarita mix, next 4 ingredients, and, if desired, tequila. Whisk (or seal bag and shake) to blend. Add chicken; cover or seal, and chill at least 2 hours or up to 6 hours. Remove chicken from marinade, discarding marinade. Set chicken aside.
2. Prepare rice according to package directions; keep warm.
3. Coat cold cooking grate of grill with cooking spray, and place on grill. Preheat grill to 300° to 350° (medium) heat. Place chicken on grate.
4. Grill chicken, covered with grill lid, 6 minutes on each side or until done. Serve over hot cooked rice. Serve with Mango Salsa.

Mango Salsa

MAKES about 2½ cups • **HANDS-ON TIME:** 10 min. • **TOTAL TIME:** 10 min.

- 2 mangoes, peeled
- 2 avocados, peeled
- 1 red bell pepper
- ½ red onion
- 1 Tbsp. chopped fresh cilantro
- 1 Tbsp. vegetable oil
- Juice of 1 large lime (about 1 Tbsp.)

1. Chop mangoes, avocados, red bell pepper, and red onion; place in a medium bowl. Add chopped cilantro, oil, and lime juice. Chill, if desired.

Grilled Chicken-and-Veggie Tortellini

Grilled Chicken-and-Veggie Tortellini

kids' favorite

MAKES 4 servings • **HANDS-ON TIME:** 22 min. • **TOTAL TIME:** 32 min.

- 4 small zucchini, cut in half lengthwise (about 1¼ lb.)
- 2 skinned and boned chicken breasts (13 oz.)
- 1 Tbsp. freshly ground Italian herb seasoning (we tested with McCormick Italian Herb Seasoning Grinder)
- 1 (19-oz.) package frozen cheese-filled tortellini
- 1 (7-oz.) container refrigerated reduced-fat pesto
- 2 large tomatoes, seeded and chopped

1. Preheat grill to 300° to 350° (medium) heat. Sprinkle zucchini and chicken with seasoning.
2. Grill zucchini and chicken at the same time, covered with grill lid. Grill zucchini 6 to 8 minutes on each side or until tender. Grill chicken 5 to 6 minutes on each side or until done. Remove from grill; let stand 10 minutes.
3. Meanwhile, prepare tortellini according to package directions. Coarsely chop chicken and zucchini. Toss tortellini with pesto, tomatoes, chicken, and zucchini. Serve immediately.

Chicken-Blueberry Salad

MAKES 4 servings • **HANDS-ON TIME:** 32 min. • **TOTAL TIME:** 1 hr., 32 min.

- ½ cup rice wine vinegar
- 3 Tbsp. olive oil
- 2 tsp. minced fresh ginger
- ½ tsp. black pepper
- ¼ tsp. salt
- 1 garlic clove, minced
- 3 skinned and boned chicken breast halves
- 1 celery rib, chopped
- 1 cup shredded carrots
- ½ cup sweet onion, diced
- ½ cup red bell pepper, chopped
- 4 cups torn mixed salad greens
- 1 cup fresh blueberries

1. Whisk together first 6 ingredients. Reserve half of mixture, and chill.
2. Place chicken in a shallow dish or zip-top plastic freezer bag; pour remaining mixture over chicken. Cover or seal, and chill at least 1 hour.
3. Preheat grill to 350° to 400° (medium-high) heat. Remove chicken from marinade; discard marinade. Grill chicken 6 minutes on each side or until done. Cut into thin slices.
4. Combine celery and next 3 ingredients; add reserved dressing, tossing to coat.
5. Place chicken over greens. Top with celery mixture; sprinkle with berries.

Grilled Vegetable Pasta

To hold the onions together on the grill, insert a wooden pick through each slice.

MAKES 4 servings • **HANDS-ON TIME:** 30 min. • **TOTAL TIME:** 30 min.

- 4 tomatoes, cut into 1-inch slices
- 1 onion, cut into slices
- 1 zucchini, cut in half lengthwise
- 1 yellow squash, cut in half lengthwise
- 2 garlic cloves, minced
- 2 Tbsp. olive oil
- ½ tsp. salt
- ¼ tsp. freshly ground pepper
- 8 oz. penne, cooked
- ¼ cup chopped fresh basil
- ½ cup freshly grated Parmesan cheese

1. Preheat grill to 350° to 400° (medium-high) heat. Toss together first 8 ingredients in a large bowl.
2. Grill vegetables, covered with grill lid, turning occasionally, 6 minutes or until tender.
3. Cut zucchini and squash halves into thin slices, and place in a large bowl. Add remaining grilled vegetables, pasta, and basil, tossing gently; sprinkle with cheese.

Grilled Tomato-Rosemary Tart

Serve this savory pie as a starter for a ladies' gathering, or have it as a light supper with a tossed salad.

MAKES 4 servings • **HANDS-ON TIME:** 15 min. • **TOTAL TIME:** 57 min.

- 3 plum tomatoes
- ½ tsp. kosher salt
- ½ (17.3-oz.) package frozen puff pastry sheets, thawed
- ¼ cup (2 oz.) shredded mozzarella cheese
- 1 tsp. lemon zest
- 1 tsp. fresh rosemary
- ½ tsp. freshly ground pepper

1. Preheat oven to 400°. Cut tomatoes into ¼-inch slices, and place on a paper towel-lined wire rack. Sprinkle tomatoes with salt. Let stand 20 minutes. Pat dry with paper towels.
2. Unfold 1 puff pastry sheet on a lightly floured baking sheet. Arrange tomato slices in a single layer on pastry. Stir together cheese and next 3 ingredients in a small bowl. Sprinkle cheese mixture over tomatoes.
3. Preheat grill to 350° to 400° (medium-high) heat. Turn 1 side of grill off; leave other side lit. Transfer tart from baking sheet to unlit side of grill, and grill, covered with grill lid, 20 to 22 minutes or until pastry is puffed and golden brown.

Grilled Tomato-Rosemary Tart

menus

New Orleans Dinner
Serves 4

Cajun Omelet, page 14
Green salad
French bread

Fast and Fresh
Serves 6

Farmers Market Scramble, page 24
Fresh fruit
Biscuits

Breakfast for Dinner
Serves 4

Guiltless French Toast, page 41
Bacon strips
Mixed fresh berries

Pasta Supper
Serves 2 to 3

Bow-Tie Pasta Toss, page 69
Spinach salad
Garlic breadsticks

Weekend Dinner
Serves 6

Quick 'n' Easy Chicken Barbecue Pizza, page 58
Carrot and celery sticks
Ice cream sundaes

Summer Menu
Serves 6

Grilled Tomato-Peach Pizza, page 52
Watermelon slices
Bakery lemon bars

Tex-Mex Supper
Serves 4 to 6

Easy Skillet Tacos, page 92
Sliced melon
Mexican brownies

Southern Supper
Serves 4

Spicy Catfish with Vegetables and Basil Cream, page 114
Coleslaw
Hush puppies

Stir-Fry Supper
Serves 4

Garlic Turkey-Broccoli Stir-Fry, page 113
Orange wedges
Crusty rolls

Game Day Menu
Serves 6 to 8

Quick Turkey Chili, page 143
Assorted fresh vegetables with dip
Soup crackers

Autumn Menu

Serves 8

Harvest Lamb Stew, page 140
Coleslaw
Crusty rolls

Simple Weeknight Dinner

Serves 4

Pork Tenderloin and Tomato Salad, page 153
Marinated asparagus
Dinner rolls

Italian Dinner

Serves 6 to 8

Spinach-Ravioli Lasagna, page 171
Caesar salad
Garlic bread

Kids' Favorite Dinner

Serves 6

Pizza Spaghetti Casserole, page 187
Apple slices
Chocolate chip cookies

Home-Style Dinner

Serves 8 to 10

Classic Chicken Tetrazzini, page 175
Tossed green salad
Apple crisp

Indoor Barbecue

Serves 12

Slow-Cooker Barbecue Beef Sandwiches, page 214
Baked beans
Coleslaw

Creole Classic

Serves 10

Slow-Cooker Red Beans and Rice, page 237
Spinach salad
French bread

Southern Comfort Food

Serves 4 to 6

Pot Roast with Vegetables, page 257
Coleslaw
Crusty rolls

Irish Dinner

Serves 6

Corned Beef and Cabbage, page 258
Steamed carrots
Irish soda bread

Fiesta Night

Serves 6

Beef Fajitas with Pico de Gallo, page 296
Guacamole salad
Lime sherbet

Backyard Burger Bash

Serves 4

Bacon-Wrapped Barbecue Burgers, page 288
Chips
Bakery brownies

Skewer Supper

Serves 4 to 6

Spicy Glazed Shrimp Kabobs, page 279
Yellow rice
Cantaloupe

metric equivalents

The recipes that appear in this cookbook use the standard U.S. method for measuring liquid and dry or solid ingredients (teaspoons, tablespoons, and cups). The information in the following charts is provided to help cooks outside the United States successfully use these recipes. All equivalents are approximate.

Metric Equivalents for Different Types of Ingredients

A standard cup measure of a dry or solid ingredient will vary in weight depending on the type of ingredient. A standard cup of liquid is the same volume for any type of liquid. Use the following chart when converting standard cup measures to grams (weight) or milliliters (volume).

Standard Cup	Fine Powder (ex. flour)	Grain (ex. rice)	Granular (ex. sugar)	Liquid Solids (ex. butter)	Liquid (ex. milk)
1	140 g	150 g	190 g	200 g	240 ml
¾	105 g	113 g	143 g	150 g	180 ml
⅔	93 g	100 g	125 g	133 g	160 ml
½	70 g	75 g	95 g	100 g	120 ml
⅓	47 g	50 g	63 g	67 g	80 ml
¼	35 g	38 g	48 g	50 g	60 ml
⅛	18 g	19 g	24 g	25 g	30 ml

Useful Equivalents for Liquid Ingredients by Volume

¼ tsp							=	1 ml
½ tsp							=	2 ml
1 tsp							=	5 ml
3 tsp	=	1 Tbsp			=	½ fl oz	=	15 ml
		2 Tbsp	=	⅛ cup	=	1 fl oz	=	30 ml
		4 Tbsp	=	¼ cup	=	2 fl oz	=	60 ml
		5⅓ Tbsp	=	⅓ cup	=	3 fl oz	=	80 ml
		8 Tbsp	=	½ cup	=	4 fl oz	=	120 ml
		10⅔ Tbsp	=	⅔ cup	=	5 fl oz	=	160 ml
		12 Tbsp	=	¾ cup	=	6 fl oz	=	180 ml
		16 Tbsp	=	1 cup	=	8 fl oz	=	240 ml
		1 pt	=	2 cups	=	16 fl oz	=	480 ml
		1 qt	=	4 cups	=	32 fl oz	=	960 ml
						33 fl oz	=	1000 ml

Useful Equivalents for Dry Ingredients by Weight

(To convert ounces to grams, multiply the number of ounces by 30.)

1 oz	=	1/16 lb	=	30 g
4 oz	=	¼ lb	=	120 g
8 oz	=	½ lb	=	240 g
12 oz	=	¾ lb	=	360 g
16 oz	=	1 lb	=	480 g

Useful Equivalents for Length

(To convert inches to centimeters, multiply the number of inches by 2.5.)

1 in					=	2.5 cm		
6 in	=	½ ft			=	15 cm		
12 in	=	1 ft			=	30 cm		
36 in	=	3 ft	=	1 yd	=	90 cm		
40 in					=	100 cm	=	1 m

Useful Equivalents for Cooking/Oven Temperatures

	Fahrenheit	Celsius	Gas Mark
Freeze water	32° F	0° C	
Room temperature	68° F	20° C	
Boil water	212° F	100° C	
Bake	325° F	160° C	3
	350° F	180° C	4
	375° F	190° C	5
	400° F	200° C	6
	425° F	220° C	7
	450° F	230° C	8
Broil			Grill

index